"*You Welcomed Me* invites us into the amazing oppor⌐⌐⌐⌐ ⌐⌐⌐⌐ and immigrants. We get to love others because God first loved us. We get to welcome Christ into our lives because 'I was a stranger and you welcomed me.' We get to witness for Jesus when we're known for loving our vulnerable neighbors. This book inspires, addresses concerns, and gives wise, practical advice for you and your church. Fear and politics can distract us, but *You Welcomed Me* is a compassionate call to make much of love and make much of Jesus in our lives."

Ed Stetzer, Billy Graham Distinguished Chair at Wheaton College

"Fear is the enemy of love. When fear rather than love is the driving force behind our life choices and public policies, we end up contributing to the suffering of the world rather than alleviating it. Kent's new book *You Welcomed Me* stands firmly on the biblical promise that perfect love casts out fear. He reminds us that when we welcome the stranger we welcome Christ . . . and when we do not welcome the stranger, we do not welcome Christ. Quite simply, this is an invitation to love like Jesus loves—with arms wide open— and to be as hospitable to others as God has been to us."

Shane Claiborne, author and activist, director of Red Letter Christians, founder of The Simple Way, author of *Beating Guns*

"Kent Annan is a gifted storyteller. *You Welcomed Me* vividly conveys the stories of refugees and other immigrants throughout the world, challenging preconceptions and inviting readers to consider how the lives of displaced people might intersect with our own stories and, ultimately, with God's story. A compelling, inspiring look at one of the most pressing issues of our day."

Matthew Soerens, US director of church mobilization, World Relief, and national coordinator, Evangelical Immigration Table, coauthor of *Welcoming the Stranger* and *Seeking Refuge*

"*You Welcomed Me* is a must-read challenge to greater involvement and action on behalf of refugees coming to our country. Kent Annan surrounds us with stories, information, and highly accessible action plans, but this book stands alone. Unlike any other book on the subject, Kent provokes us to look inward—to examine our own hearts, our self-interests, our fears, and our understanding of God's love and mercy. *You Welcomed Me* invites the reader to greater involvement, but it first looks to transform our hearts."

Paul Borthwick, senior consultant, Development Associates International, author of *Great Commission, Great Compassion*

"The issue of refugees and immigrants has become so politicized in our culture with narratives of fear and protectionism often drowning out the facts and the sheer humanity of their plight. Amazingly, we might even miss the key truth behind the question, what would Jesus do? That's why this thoughtful book by Kent Annan is so necessary now, to share stories and insights through the lens of Scripture. Read it as a tool to engage—because as Christ-followers we must engage in the most urgent humanitarian crisis of our lifetime."
Rich Stearns, World Vision US president, author of *The Hole in Our Gospel*

"Annan cuts through the complexities around refugees, immigrants, and politics to create a compelling call for God's people to welcome refugees in meaningful ways. *You Welcomed Me* is an essential tool for those who want to get beyond the headlines and do something. With tangible, practical steps, Annan takes insights about bias, power, and 'othering' and creates steps to cultivate prophetic hospitality to the stranger."
Nikki Toyama-Szeto, executive director of Evangelicals for Social Action/ The Sider Center

"Kent Annan is a masterful writer and thoughtful, compassionate humanitarian who knows how to love in word and deed. His life service matches his lip service and the words on the pages of this book. These words are clothed in the love of God that welcomes the stranger, refugee, and immigrant, in not only theoretical ways but through meaningful, practical suggestions. This book is 'for such a time as this,' a prophetic literary witness of the gospel for today. If you want to be more like Jesus, if you want to know the welcoming presence of God for the least, the lost, and the left out, read this book because in its pages breathes the hospitality of God for all people. In it, the reader will be challenged not only to be for Jesus but to be for what Jesus was for."
Luke Powery, dean of Duke University Chapel, associate professor of homiletics, Duke Divinity School

"*You Welcomed Me* is an urgent book that is inspiring, practical, and deeply rooted in spiritual practice. We're beloved by God and so we're welcomed and we're freed to welcome the stranger, the refugee, and the immigrant. Justice issues are also issues of our spirit, and God's generous presence transforms how we see others. In *You Welcomed Me*, Annan invites the reader into the freedom and responsibility of a deeper relationship with Jesus and with our neighbors. This is an essential invitation into a divine, loving way of life."
Richard Rohr, founder of the Center for Action and Contemplation

"*You Welcomed Me* is the book the church needs now to respond to the world with love. This conversation about welcome led by Kent Annan is necessary, helpful, and hopeful. This small volume provides space for good conversations that do not simplify or ignore the complexities of refugee resettlement, immigration, or security. Readers can learn and find new paths forward with practices that teach us to take the next steps in welcoming. It is easy to be overwhelmed, but *You Welcomed Me* will leave you filled with hope for how you can embody God's generous welcome in our world!"

Kelley Nikondeha, author of *Adopted*

"Kent gently provokes the reader toward inner contemplation and outward praxis in regard to a gospel-infused perspective on refugees and immigrants. In sharing actual stories based on his own proximity, he enlightens us on the biblical call of welcoming and empowering refugees alongside the necessary work of recognizing universal brokenness, beginning first with ourselves. *You Welcomed Me* is an important work for a crucial time in America's history."

Gena Thomas, author of *A Smoldering Wick*

"At a moment when Americans struggle with a global migration debate beamed into their living rooms and onto their phones, *You Welcomed Me* provides a path forward. Drawing on Scripture, Kent describes two things. One, why people decide they must leave their homes. And two, why living up to our responsibility to welcome the stranger is difficult. *You Welcomed Me* is honest, compassionate, and pragmatic—well worth your reading and reflection."

Ali Noorani, executive director of the National Immigration Forum, author of *There Goes the Neighborhood*

"Kent Annan masterfully takes the reader on a journey of empathy and understanding regarding, first of all, what God is doing in our hearts in relation to how we treat and welcome immigrants and refugees. Instead of focusing on fear and protecting ourselves, Kent asks us to consider how our hearts and lives might be shaped by God through the practice of welcoming the stranger. If we consider our neighbor as fully human, made in God's image, and deeply loved by God, how might our reaction change? How might we change? This book is a spiritual journey through the blessing of welcoming where we find that we are the ones who truly benefit."

Alan Cross, Southern Baptist minister, author of *When Heaven and Earth Collide*

"In this book, Kent Annan generously opens up the conversation about refugees and immigrants to create space for real listening and honest self-reflection. It continually reminds the reader of the costs—spiritual, economic, and social—of choosing to close our hearts to the stranger in the age of the exile. As a person who has continuously been welcomed by refugees in my own neighborhood, this book will be one I recommend over and over again to people who long to love their neighbors—both global and local—as themselves."

D. L. Mayfield, activist, author of *Assimilate or Go Home*

"According to Jesus hospitality is a defining feature of genuine Christianity. This book will inspire, equip, and challenge us all toward authentic discipleship. I urge you to read it."

Krish Kandiah, author of *God Is Stranger*

YOU WELCOMED ME

LOVING REFUGEES AND IMMIGRANTS BECAUSE GOD FIRST LOVED US

KENT ANNAN

IVP Books

An imprint of InterVarsity Press
Downers Grove, Illinois

InterVarsity Press
P.O. Box 1400, Downers Grove, IL 60515-1426
ivpress.com
email@ivpress.com

InterVarsity Press® is the book-publishing division of InterVarsity Christian Fellowship/USA®, a movement of students and faculty active on campus at hundreds of universities, colleges, and schools of nursing in the United States of America, and a member movement of the International Fellowship of Evangelical Students. For information about local and regional activities, visit intervarsity.org.

Published in association with Creative Trust Literary Group LLC, 210 Jamestown Park Drive, Suite 200, Brentwood, TN 37027, www.creativetrust.com.

Cover design: David Fassett
Interior design: Daniel van Loon
Images: wooden floor: © Sutasinee Anukul / EyeEm / Getty Images
*   retro corner art: © Extezy / iStock / Getty Images Plus*
*   paper background: © duncan1890 / iStock / Getty Images Plus*

ISBN 978-0-8308-4553-8 (print)
ISBN 978-0-8308-7377-7 (digital)

Printed in the United States of America ♾

InterVarsity Press is committed to ecological stewardship and to the conservation of natural resources in all our operations. This book was printed using sustainably sourced paper.

Library of Congress Cataloging-in-Publication Data
Names: Annan, Kent, 1973- author.
Title: You welcomed me : loving refugees and immigrants because God first loved us / Kent Annan.
Description: Downers Grove : InterVarsity Press, 2018.
Identifiers: LCCN 2018028341 (print) | LCCN 2018034437 (ebook) | ISBN 9780830873777 (eBook) | ISBN 9780830845538 (pbk. : alk. paper)
Subjects: LCSH: Hospitality--Religious aspects--Christianity. | Church work with refugees. | Church work with immigrants. | Emigration and immigration--Religious aspects--Christianity.
Classification: LCC BV4647.H67 (ebook) | LCC BV4647.H67 A56 2018 (print) | DDC 261.8/328--dc23
LC record available at https://lccn.loc.gov/2018028341

P	21	20	19	18	17	16	15	14	13	12	11	10	9	8	7	6	5	4	3	2
Y	36	35	34	33	32	31	30	29	28	27	26	25	24	23	22	21	20	19

Simone and Cormac, this book is dedicated to you.

I'm grateful every day that I got to welcome you into the world

as your dad. I'm grateful for who you are and

who you are becoming.

We love because [God] first loved us.

1 JOHN 4:19

If we are to love our neighbors, before doing anything else we must see our neighbors. With our imagination as well as our eyes . . . we must see not just their faces but the life behind and within their faces.

FREDERICK BUECHNER

✢ CONTENTS ✢

ARE WE FOR
OR AGAINST?

*The ache for home lives in all of us, the safe place
where we can go as we are and not be questioned.*

MAYA ANGELOU,
ALL GOD'S CHILDREN NEED TRAVELING SHOES

*D*o you remember what it means when people are
refugees or immigrants?" I ask my eight-year-old son.

"Yes, Dad. We talked about that last week. Remember?"

"I'm going to write my next book about this."

"Okay. But wait, are we *for* them or *against* them?"

"*For them.* Remember. Being a refugee means someone
had to run away from something bad, like war. They had
to leave home, leave everything behind. Can you imagine
if we had to leave our house and your school and move
somewhere far away, where they speak another language,
because we weren't safe? And an immigrant is coming to
somewhere new, which is usually hard too. We want to be
people who help people in hard situations, right?"

"Sure. But some people are *against*, right? Why?"

"I think people are nervous or scared about a few things. Safety is one. They don't want any bad people to get in who could hurt them. They also think people might take their jobs. And new people can bring change with them—like a different language, culture, or religion that they don't want."

"Okay, watch this move. You stand right there. I'm going to jump off the couch and kick you. You try to block my kick, but you won't be able to because the crane kick cannot be defended."

We'd watched the old *Karate Kid* as our family movie the night before, so 95 percent of the conversation then turned to punches, kicks, "not that hard!" and laughter. I knew the movie might put the rest of our family in danger for a few days as my son works out his new Karate Kid techniques. But as we keep talking, in between indefensible crane kicks—and in the future as he keeps getting older—I want him to recognize what is at stake:

- Love versus fear
- Who we want to be
- What home is
- How we deal with real concerns
- How we make difficult decisions about responding to other people's suffering when there isn't enough for everyone to meet their own wants and needs—in this world that gives lots to some and crushes others
- Wisdom versus naiveté versus ideals
- The future of our nation
- The way ethnicity and race affect lives and relationships

How can we see those pictures of Syrian children—a boy's limp body lying face-down on a beach, a boy sitting in the back of an ambulance stunned after an explosion with his face caked in dust and blood; boys just a little younger than my son—and not forfeit some essential part of being human if we don't help? There may be some risk to helping, but there is certainly risk to not helping:

- Making *security* such a high value that *fear* gains godlike power over our lives—instead of seeing security as one important consideration among others.

- Discovering that our faith is a resounding gong, a clanging cymbal, not worth much more than empty words when it comes to the rubber of love meeting the road of suffering and sacrifice.

Yes, so much is at stake in how we respond to refugees and immigrants. Working through such complexities requires open hearts, clear thinking, and practical acts. It also requires finding ways to disagree that help us all get better together rather than just making others and ourselves worse. Above all, it requires getting to know other people who we think are different—and then finding that yes, they're different, but not so much.

I love being a dad. Besides spontaneous karate battles with my son, I keep finding that my kids expose my generosity and my hypocrisy, my love and my selfishness. They reflect myself back to me. What we model is more important than what we say.

How we answer my son's question, "Are we *for* or *against* them?" reveals a lot about what kind of family, community, and country we want to be. After the answer comes the work to understand the nuances and navigate the complexity. As adults, we know there is usually a cost to being our best selves—and that it's ultimately worth the price.

How can we live into a vision that chooses love over fear?

THAT COULD BE ME

After college I moved to England and then France to work with a refugee ministry for two years. A few years later, during the war in

Kosovo, I moved for six months to Albania and Kosovo to help respond to the refugee crisis there. I'd seen heart-wrenching refugee photos on the front page of the newspaper. I needed to help if I could.

Friendships and working with refugees changed my life's direction. I had Turkish coffee with Kosovar families who had fled, leaving behind their dead husbands and sons as well as the charred remains of their homes that had been burned to the ground. Later I pushed a wheelbarrow filled with a family's only possessions as they boarded a bus to Kosovo to restart from nothing.

In France I lived in a hostel with refugees from Sierra Leone and Sarajevo, both places that experienced violent conflicts. We became friends and ate dinners together. Once I got lucky and beat the guy from Sarajevo in chess. He said he'd fought in the war there before escaping. The other fifty times he beat me.

One morning near Christmas, snow started falling. It was the first time the guys from Sierra Leone had ever seen snow. We all ran outside. We slid up and down the road, laughing and falling like kindergartners. The guy from Sarajevo also asked me to help him buy a bottle of rum because he needed help to sleep at night. There was laughter, but the shadow of loss they'd each endured always lurked nearby.

These guys were around my age. My experience with them transformed me because the distance between us/them, between you/me collapsed. I could have been the one who had to leave everything and everyone and hope for mercy along the way.

I want my son to see that we're *for* them. I want my son to see *we could be them*. I want my son to hear that Jesus said to love our neighbors as ourselves. Inspiring, demanding words to live by. These words invite us to embrace our common humanity and risk love.

"That could be me" at face value can be a selfish formulation. But it can also lead our imaginations down the path toward deeper empathy and love—because it recognizes the stranger as ourselves and helps us choose to be *for*.

4

That could be me unable to find work, so my child can't go to school and his hair is turning rust-colored because of malnutrition. I've walked along dirt paths and talked with dads and moms in Haiti who give all they can to provide for their children, and it's not nearly enough. I saw them move to the Dominican Republic to work awful jobs cutting sugar cane, never seeing their families so they could support their families.

That could be me having to leave my family behind, crossing a border and a desert to work grueling days picking tomatoes or strawberries in the Florida sun, hunched over doing work nobody local would do, so I can send money back to my children who I don't get to see for months on end.

That could be me without a home, without a place that isn't haunted by fear and uncertainty.

That could be me, one of the Syrian refugees in whose home I sat drinking tea in Mafraq, Jordan. They lost their home, left all they had behind. They also talked, four years into being refugees, about how hard it was without full rights to work or start a business in their host country when they had lost everything. Though they longed to return, they had no idea if or when they'd go back to Syria—and meanwhile weren't really even able to start over. On average, refugees are away from their home country for more than ten years.

That could be me loving my neighbor as myself—and discovering that in the deepest sense we're all exiles trying to find home. Following Jesus means to some extent confessing that we don't have a permanent home here. We want to belong most of all to God's kingdom coming. We're also to live with an eye to helping widows and orphans out on the margins. This isn't liberal wishy-washiness or conservative literalism. This is the rigorous life of love worth living, love that opens the world to us, that leads us toward discovery and transformation. It leads toward the discomfort of growth. We carry the weight of caring and then find our hearts grow stronger.

THE CRISIS AND OPPORTUNITY

We're in a crisis—nationally, globally, and existentially—because 66 million people have been forced from their homes:

- 44 million of them are displaced within their own countries.

- 22 million had to flee their country as refugees because of persecution, war, or violence.

This crisis is a large-scale version of times when a friend or neighbor has an emergency. The victim is in crisis, and a crisis is also forced on people to decide whether and how to help. Over half of these refugees are children less than eighteen years old. Their lives ask us: *Will you welcome me?* We're also in a crisis because of how immigrants and asylum seekers are being treated at and within our borders—including around three thousand children who were separated from their parents.

A refugee is someone who has been forced to flee his or her country because of persecution, war, or violence. A refugee has a well-founded fear of persecution for reasons of race, religion, nationality, political opinion, or membership in a particular social group. Most likely, they cannot return home or are afraid to do so.

The United States has been granting legal residency to about 1 million immigrants a year, which includes welcoming about 75,000 refugees. Now the US is slated to receive fewer than 22,000 refugees, the lowest number in decades. The countries that currently welcome the largest number of refugees are places with conflict near their borders: Turkey, Pakistan, Lebanon, Iran, Ethiopia, and Jordan, who each have welcomed between 650,000 and 2.5 million refugees. In other words, these much-smaller countries are receiving between 30 and 113 times *more* refugees than we are.

Statistics can numb us. Compassion fatigue can drain us because we don't know what to do in the face of these numbers and complexities for people so far away. So the spiritual/existential crisis for us is this: How can we *not* ignore the people behind these numbers and not let our tribal instincts (take care of our own!) or our fear (terrorists or gang members are hiding among them!) keep us from loving well and wisely?

In early 2017, in the weeks after the new presidential administration put a travel ban on immigrants and refugees from seven countries in the Middle East, statistics and policies became freshly personal. Whether and how to welcome strangers across our borders briefly became the biggest topic of national conversation. At the time, the *Washington Post* told the story of refugees in Nebraska, which leans politically conservative and has taken more refugees per capita than any other state.

"I hated Muslims," said sixty-one-year-old John Dutcher about his post-9/11 mindset. His mind changed after Muslim refugee families moved into his apartment complex.

"The Muslims here were all about family and they just loved everyone," he said. "I remember the people who lived here before; they took for granted everything this country gave them. These people, they really changed my heart."

He had learned their stories of fleeing war in Syria and losing everything. They shared meals with him. He felt safer around them than around the previous tenants.

An immigrant is someone who has moved to another country for reasons that could include fleeing violence, natural disaster, or extreme poverty. They could be reuniting with family or looking for education or opportunity for themselves and their families. Refugees are a category of immigrants who have fled under specific circumstances.

Dutcher didn't initially welcome them, but together they eventually found their way to welcoming each other. Where fear and hate close possibilities, love opens new opportunities. Where darkness takes hold, light has opportunity to shine more brightly.

Where violence tears apart, connection can heal. Our lives can overflow with precisely this light, generosity, and healing—when instead of ignoring suffering, we open ourselves to love. Then life gets so much better: their lives and our lives. (As an economic example of new opportunities, about 40 percent of Fortune 500 companies were started by immigrants or their children.)

Ali Al Sudani's story was told in *Texas Monthly* around this same time. He's the exact same age as I am; *we could have been each other*. But he grew up in Iraq as part of "the War Children" generation through the Iran-Iraq war. In 2003 he became a translator for British soldiers, a connection that eventually made him unsafe. He became a refugee in Jordan. In 2009 he arrived in Houston, alone.

Since then he has become director of refugee services for Interfaith Ministries, helping others who have to restart in Houston. Based on the total number (not per capita), Texas resettles more refugees than any other state. As he helps, Sudani knows firsthand how hard it is to start over from scratch in a strange land. He likes to quote Jesus in the Gospel of Matthew: "I was a stranger and you welcomed me" (Matthew 25:35). Sudani was welcomed, and now he welcomes.

Jesus taught us how to see each other. God's love welcomes us, so we want to welcome others. In a way that is gritty and practical but also kind of mystical, welcoming the stranger is also welcoming God—in our tender frailty and shared sorrow, in our courageous resiliency and remarkable generosity, in our fierce commitment to finding ways forward. In the deepest sense, we have an opportunity to do nothing less than to find a way—even when it isn't easy—to welcome each other and God into our lives.

We welcome, knowing it's not simple, aware that things big and small can go wrong, grappling with complex issues to navigate. We welcome a better version of ourselves. We welcome a new story, new life. We find beauty and hope in welcoming each other.

TESTIFYING TO GOD'S KINGDOM

In this book, I hope to inspire you with stories of refugees and immigrants and those who are involved with them. I hope to inform you with research, sacred text, and experiences. I hope for nothing less than seeing our—and other people's—lives changed along the way.

We all struggle, one way or another, with dislocation, loss, and anxiety over what faces us. We're people of faith, however, seekers, children of Abraham's faith. By faith we've joined into the story that we're in a sense foreigners ourselves, and so we should be especially sensitive to those who are displaced and seeking a way home. In our deepest hope, we're sojourners ourselves, which should lead us into a special tenderness for the plight of foreigners.

Hebrews 11 tells us that the forebears of our faith "confessed that they were strangers and foreigners on the earth, for people who speak in this way make it clear that they are seeking a homeland. . . . They desire a better country, that is, a heavenly one. Therefore God is not ashamed to be called their God; indeed, he has prepared a city for them" (Hebrews 11:13-16).

Yes, we desire that homeland, that kingdom of God—and also that this kingdom of God would, as Jesus prayed, come on earth as in heaven. So in the next chapter we look at why we should be *for* refugees and immigrants: they're fellow children of God, whom we recognize as ourselves and who are in need. This leads us to empathy and love (chapter 2).

Once we see the need and start to recognize them as ourselves, we'll reflect on fears, complexities, and barriers that can keep us from being as welcoming as possible. We'll name these concerns honestly so that we can seek truth and follow where God's love leads (chapter 3).

That prepares us to listen deeply to experiences of refugees and immigrants who invite us to be part of their stories and to live a better story ourselves (chapter 4).

Recognizing the need, understanding our connection, addressing our concerns, and being inspired by their stories all leads, of course, to action. There are good, practical ways we can help locally, nationally, and internationally—as an individual, family, school, or church (chapter 5).

We'll then see what commitments will help us keep on loving and learning together (chapter 6). Finally, we'll conclude with a vision for how life is deeper, better, and more faithful together (chapter 7).

Think about what the following two phrases would say about your life:

To have to flee your home and your homeland. These words testify to trauma none of us ever wants to face.

You welcomed me. These words testify to doing justice, loving kindness, and walking humbly with God—words that could go on the tombstone of a life well lived. In helping to give the homeless a new home, we bring ourselves closer to Home. We become part of the kingdom, coming.

PRACTICE

Responding Within God's Love for Us

At the end of each chapter I suggest one or two practices to help you reflect on and put the chapter's ideas into action. Each of these practices is rooted in grace and empathy, in relationship and hope.

The two practices for this chapter are ways to affirm that we want love to guide us not the agenda of politicians, newscasters, or clickbait headlines. Instead we want to be guided by God's agenda, which includes unfailing love for us.

These practices are inspired by a traditional form of prayer called the *examen*, in which we look back over the day and see where love flowed through us and where it was blocked. We approach this not judging ourselves or others but listening with honesty, grace, and faith so the Spirit can move in and through us. For each of these, I suggest taking about ten minutes to sit quietly and go through the steps.

Practice one: How we react to refugees and immigrants.

- First, become aware of God's presence. God loves you and welcomes you in your wonderfulness, brokenness, selfishness, fear, and beauty. You are welcome in God's presence.

- Review the experience of what it would be like if you became a refugee. You can move through being grateful that you aren't facing this, and then imagine having to leave everything behind and move away. You lose your home, your kids' school, and your job and have to move to Mexico with only what you can carry. You start over in a new land, unable to speak the language, without connections to help you. What might it be like for you to become a refugee?

- Pay attention to your emotions. Don't judge yourself. The Spirit is with you. See what you feel. *That could be me,* and we're slowing down to consider that reality. What would the experience be like? What would be hardest to lose? We don't presume to understand what it is like, but we can listen to their lives and let our imaginations be guided along the way of love and empathy.

- Choose one aspect of the experience—what you thought or imagined—that rose to the top for you. Was it losing your house, not being able to communicate, the way all security (financial, physical) disappeared, the uncertainty, the stress of caring for loved ones, or something else? Now pray for people who are in those situations. You don't know their names or the specifics of what they find hardest, but God does.

- Look toward tomorrow, guided by the reality that you are beloved and you are called to love. Amen.

Practice two: How to understand your own reaction.

- First, become aware of God's presence. God loves you and welcomes you in your wonderfulness, brokenness, selfishness, fear, and beauty. You are welcome in God's presence.

- As you came into this book, or when the issue of refugees or immigrants comes up in the media or in conversation, where do you find your spirit responding *for* refugees and immigrants, and where does it respond *against*? This is private. There are legitimate concerns. There are also fears that might surprise you as a bit ugly. You don't have to post any of this on Facebook. You're invited to be honest with God and yourself. What reaction do you find in yourself toward refugees and immigrants? Where does love flow freely? What makes you feel resistance?

- Now spend time thinking about where your love for immigrants and refugees flows freely, and feel grateful for that flow. Then consider areas where love feels blocked by some sort of fear or objection and take time with God to pay attention to the emotion or argument and understand why. We pay attention by asking the Spirit to help us to see the reasons. They might be valid reasons or they might not be. Ultimately we want God's love guiding us.

- Choose one aspect of the uncomfortable or love-blocking feelings or thoughts that rose to the top and pray that God would guide you in the way of welcoming. This doesn't mean agreeing with someone else's agenda or winning or losing a debate. You're simply welcoming God to show you where you might be guided in the way of God's welcoming love.

- Look toward tomorrow, guided by the reality that you are beloved and you are called to love. Amen.

THAT
COULD BE ME

We are all strangers in a strange land, longing for home, but not quite knowing what or where home is.

MADELEINE L'ENGLE

*L*aura woke up at 5:00 a.m. to drive in the dark cold of a Wisconsin winter to the airport. She did this often as a Fortune 1000 executive.

As she sat on the plane ready for a short nap and then preparing for meetings in Washington, DC, that afternoon, a group of tall young women boarded: the Georgetown University women's basketball team. A player sat next to her. They talked briefly. The team lost last night, which made the early flight home even less enjoyable.

They were buckled in when a different Georgetown player came down the aisle and asked her teammate seated next to Laura, "This looks like a really nice lady you're next to. Do you mind if I trade seats with you?"

At this point many of us would be on alert, thinking, "Uh-oh, someone needy is going to be invading my private space."

She sat down next to Laura and, nervous and jittery, explained she doesn't do well flying.

Laura is very kind but also from the Midwest, where friendliness tends to be reserved. She felt compelled to ask something she'd never asked a stranger before: "Do you want to say a prayer?"

"That would be great," said the basketball player.

Laura instinctively offered her hand as they prayed. They held hands for takeoff. Then they kept holding hands, without saying a word to each other, for the rest of the flight until they landed safely.

We recognize Laura's prayer and her hand in that moment as a connection of grace. Laura welcomed the basketball player in all her humanity, which, pre-takeoff, was dominated by her fears.

"God knows," Laura said that night reflecting on the simple holiness of the experience, "there have been times when I could have used someone's hand to comfort me on a plane—and many other times in my life. It was amazing to be there for someone when she needed it and see I could actually help."

Do we hear this and think: "Oh, whew, glad I never helped anyone in their moment of vulnerable need! What a waste of time. Laura would have done better to avoid eye contact, wear headphones, and stare down at her work. I'd never want to be a person who helped someone through a difficult moment."

No. We recognize the moment as life being beautifully lived. It's also usually more complicated than this to help someone through his or her vulnerable, fearful moments. So it's important to ask ourselves: How can we *recognize* the stranger—and then connect and help— when they don't sit next to us on a plane and personally share their needs with us?

How, if they don't reach out their hand? If their accent makes their English hard to understand? If they don't stand out as a six-foot-two female basketball player walking down the aisle? If they don't make it into the news or we don't see them day to day? In order to hear

"You welcomed me" from the people who need it most, we first have to recognize them.

WELCOMING GOD

Years ago on the other side of the world, with nobody paying attention at all, a young couple found out their child was at risk from a hostile, dangerous government. They lived in the Middle East. Life under an occupying force hadn't been a clear and present danger in their lives recently. Until now. Especially for children. No good choices. Just go. Fast. Escape. Leave behind hopes and dreams, home and work, friends and family.

They fled in the middle of the night. They took what they could carry and made it across the border. They'd left immediate danger, but that didn't mean they felt safe. They longed to be home, but to protect their child's life they couldn't.

This is a refugee story familiar to families who have fled Aleppo or South Sudan or Myanmar or many other places. It's the story of a family fleeing Guatemala or Honduras to seek asylum and protect their children from violence. The story is much too familiar for millions of mothers and fathers, sons and daughters.

This is also the refugee story of Jesus and his parents—who under the threat of a ruler named Herod had to flee to Egypt to save Jesus' life.

By recognizing strangers as ourselves and responding to their needs, we enter into one of the most simple, profound, and mysterious aspects of our faith: When we welcome refugees and immigrants, we welcome God. And when we see an immigrant or refugee in need, we see God in need. The God who loves us and gives us life also, in a way, needs our help.

"He defended the cause of the poor and needy, and so all went well. Is that not what it means to know me?" (Jeremiah 22:16 NIV). God asks this about strangers in the land.

As an adult, Jesus, who was poor and needy when escaping Herod's threat to Egypt as a child, makes Jeremiah's claim even more explicit and concrete: "I was hungry and you gave me food, I was thirsty and you gave me something to drink, I was a stranger and you welcomed me, I was naked and you gave me clothing, I was sick and you took care of me, I was in prison and you visited me. . . . Just as you did it to one of the least of these who are members of my family, you did it to me" (Matthew 25:35-36, 40).

So we come to recognize them like this:

My name is Faizah, and I am your sister. When you provide food for me when my family flees the famine in Yemen, you also give food to Jesus.

My name is Yonas, and I am your brother. When you give me clothes when I arrive from Ethiopia in Nebraska in the winter, you also give clothes to Jesus (who also would have been shockingly cold and possibly ready to curse this frozen ground like he did the fig tree that one time).

My name is María, and when you give me water in the Texas desert on the way to a job to provide for my family, you also give a drink to Jesus.

My name is Ihan, and when you visit me in the detention center where I'm held without my mom, you visit Jesus.

My name is Rahelamma, and I know it's hard to pronounce and my English isn't very good, but when you try your best it sounds to me and to Jesus something like "hallelujah."

In each person, in some mysterious way, we meet Jesus and so meet God—the Trinity in dynamic unity and diversity. Likewise, instead of seeing a stranger, we can learn to see another person with a kind of three-in-one vision. In that former stranger we can learn to see

- *the person*—a fellow human in distress,

- *ourselves*—because that could be me, and

- *God*—through the mystery that in the other we meet the divine.

It's inspiring how Uganda has received many refugees from southern Sudan and other countries. In 2016 they received more than any other country in the world—more than 1 million refugees—and with some of the most generous government policies anywhere. I was there in 2017 to visit with refugees and people working with them. Uganda has faced conflicts itself in recent decades that caused many people to be displaced from their homes in the north. Uganda's response to the hundreds of thousands of refugees flowing in from South Sudan seems to be saying not just "that could be me" but also "*that was us.*"

When we haven't had experiences forced on us, as in Uganda, we can still cultivate this three-in-one vision through deep listening, travel, friendships, and volunteering. We especially need this during a time of rapid global change that can trigger fear and resentment. (The next chapter will look closely at real concerns and wise responses.) We should search for ways to come together instead of being pushed apart. We need to find ways to go against any natural tribal instinct to care most about those who look like us, believe like us, eat like us, and talk like us so that we can live more into Paul's crucial statement: "There is no longer Jew or Greek, there is no longer slave or free, there is no longer male and female; for all of you are one in Christ Jesus" (Galatians 3:28).

Today in light of Jesus' story of the Good Samaritan, which redefines who our neighbor is, couldn't we also say, "There is no longer American or Syrian, no longer documented or undocumented, no longer legal or illegal, no longer immigrant or native-born, no longer foreigner or American"?

This doesn't solve the policy complexities that have to be addressed. But we're at the right starting point when we recognize—and love, as Jesus says—strangers as ourselves.

MOVING ALONG THE RIGHT SCALE

The famous Milgram psychological study can help us grow in *recognizing the stranger*. Participants at Yale University in 1961 were told they were taking part in a memory study, but actually the study was about their inclination to obey authority figures.

Each participant was set up as a teacher who had a student (who unknown to the "teacher" was really an actor). The teacher was then to give shocks to the student/actor as part of the learning process. The shocks weren't real, but the actor pretended to receive them and feel pain and even scream when the shocks got high enough. Under instructions by a director, the teacher started giving shocks at 15 volts and proceeded in increments of 15 volts up to a lethal 450 volts. Sixty-five percent of participants went all the way up to giving the lethal shock.

They went farther than anyone would have guessed because authority and social settings can profoundly influence how we see and treat others. Normal people (that is, most of us) are clearly susceptible to seeing and treating others as less than human.

"Once you press 15 volts, you are on that slippery slope of evil because it becomes easier and easier," said Phil Zimbardo, who ran the famous Stanford prison experiment. "The conclusion from the Milgram experiment should be: all evil begins with 15 volts. . . . The center of all prejudice, of all discrimination, is thinking of other people as less than human."

We're susceptible to dehumanizing others, which has been happening with increasing voltage to immigrants and refugees in our country's public discourse. When immigrants are falsely characterized as more prone to violent crime, that misconception shapes our imagination. When they're falsely labeled as the cause of our economic struggles, we see them differently. When people searching for safety (physical or economic) for their families are conflated with gang members who are called "animals," then fear pushes love further to the side. If we don't resist that narrative, we're taken down a slippery slope of seeing "foreigners" instead of "fellow human beings."

Now we'll look at two different scales—one that illustrates how we can move along a scale of loving our neighbors less, and another that shows how we can grow in loving our neighbors more.

THE DEHUMANIZING OUR NEIGHBOR SCALE

Absorb media that speaks unkindly and unfairly about foreigners. This is like giving an initial 15-volt shock. We're passive. We're not really hurting anyone. But like that first shock in the experiment, it starts us down a slippery slope.

Let a slur go uncorrected. If I'm with someone who speaks about a foreigner with a slur that I let go uncorrected, I slide a little farther toward not seeing people as I should. My best impulses get suppressed and lesser ones nourished.

Vote in a way that makes our vulnerable neighbors more vulnerable. Elections are complex decisions with many issues at stake, yet they come down to (a) this person or (b) that person. Loving our immigrant and refugee neighbors can take different strategies and different votes, but if we're looking out for self-interest and not loving our neighbors with our votes, then we're sliding a little further down this scale.

Fail to see God's image in them. In the experiment, an incredible number of the "teachers" kept shocking the "students" to the point that the "student" would have been dead—with the image of God in tatters both in the shocked and the shocker. We now see God's image-bearers as "immigrants" and "refugees" rather than people fleeing suffering to find life, like we all try to do, for themselves and their children. We see women and children as threats from Syria instead of as bearers of God's image in need of compassion and refuge. We see it's okay to separate young children from their parents when they're detained for crossing the border. We refuse to help. Part of our own humanity dies.

> "Do not neglect to show hospitality to strangers, for by doing that some have entertained angels without knowing it."
>
> *Hebrews 13:2*

What do we do when we recognize we're vulnerable to sliding down this slippery slope, with human lives at stake?

We can commit to moving in the opposite direction ("Lead us not into temptation") on what we'll call the Good Samaritan Scale, after the character in Jesus' story about generosity and compassion toward our neighbor who isn't a nearby neighbor or even of the same nationality. The opposite of giving that initial small shock to someone, an act of dehumanizing that leads to awful places, is to do small acts of loving kindness: to see someone injured by the side of the road and to pause, to hold someone's hand on a plane. Small steps lead us along the scale.

There is one refugee or person internally displaced within their own country for every 345 people worldwide. So this is a serious but not overwhelming problem. If we have the will, we have the resources to help.

THE GOOD SAMARITAN SCALE
(RECOGNIZING OUR NEIGHBOR)

Take time to see someone else as a person. I have to slow down to listen to someone's story, whether in person or in the news. In Jesus' story, the Good Samaritan first had to pay attention to someone he could have easily ignored as he passed by.

Take time to feel their circumstances. If I see someone as a person and then take the next step of empathizing, I'm opening myself to either action or guilt. I'm imagining walking in the shoes of that refugee or immigrant.

Seek a tangible way to connect, to give, to share a meal. If I help someone in a real way, that person's story can start to transform my story. The story of justice becomes *our story*. When we listen as we act compassionately, our respect for refugees and immigrants deepens and we find good ways to help.

Live into a new understanding of who my neighbor is. If I keep moving along this scale, I understand my neighbor, myself, and our relationship within the human family with new eyes. I see my neighbors through Jesus' redefinition—beyond my own race, nation, and creed—which changes how I work for justice locally, nationally, and internationally.

My friends Chris and Aimee Fritz moved to an Atlanta suburb recently. After they'd been there about a year, they put up a "Refugees Welcome" sign on their front lawn. Aimee told me she couldn't sleep that first night, not knowing if someone was going to be mad in the morning and rip it out. But it felt worth that risk to move along the Good Samaritan Scale and speak up for compassion.

The next day one neighbor said, "I'm glad you have that up. Screw anyone who disagrees."

A couple of weeks later, someone apparently disagreed. The sign was taken out of their front yard and laid up by their front door. (Mild suburban resistance, but the point was made.) Chris walked out and staked it back in the yard.

Seeing people other than our most immediate neighbors as *neighbors* disrupts the natural order of things. Which is good. Silence versus speaking out moves us along either the Dehumanizing Our Neighbor Scale or the Good Samaritan Scale.

The Fritz family is also involved with Refuge Coffee, a coffee shop in Clarkston, a small town near Atlanta that has received over forty thousand refugees in the past twenty-five years from all over the world. The Fritzes have taken steps there along the Good Samaritan Scale. They've met refugees whom the coffee shop employs as part of its mission. With their three children, they put together five thoughtful Christmas baskets of socks, snacks, and gift cards for refugees who came from countries including Myanmar and Morocco. They keep moving along the scale. Once when I visited their home they had invited refugees from Congo and Syria to join them for Easter dinner.

A different time I visited, we went together to Refuge Coffee for an evening when refugees and locals shared songs, dance, and stories with a couple hundred people to benefit hurricane victims in Houston.

My daughter wrote a note of encouragement and prayer in a card (drawings of families and the American flag in a heart) created by Syrian refugee girls to be sent to Houston flood victims.

Contrast the Fritzes, the other neighbors supporting local refugees, and even the young Syrian girls who cared about the suffering of their new neighbors in Houston with Nigel Farage, the politician who led Britain toward Brexit and a nationalism that encouraged people to look after their own: "What we're doing actually is we're returning to normality," he said in a TV interview. "You know, who in this world puts the interest of their next-door neighbor's family above the interest of [their own]?"

A powerful rhetorical question to punch home his point. But of course there is an easy answer to Farage's question: "Well, Jesus and Jesus' followers."

Brexit was for British voters to decide. For the question of whether we should love our neighbors as ourselves, Christians decide, "Yes, this is what we do."

In order to practice recognizing the stranger—with the hope that we will be recognized as people who love—we and our families, churches, and communities need to stay off the Dehumanizing Our Neighbor Scale and instead progress along the Good Samaritan Scale.

Along this scale we live into God's guidance: "When an alien resides with you in your land, you shall not oppress the alien. The alien who resides with you shall be to you as the citizen among you; you shall love the alien as yourself, for you were aliens in the land of Egypt" (Leviticus 19:33-34).

This will cost us something, but we gain so much as we move closer to hearing from our neighbor and God, "You welcomed me."

RECOGNIZING LOVE IN EACH OTHER

"At crucial moments of choice most of the business of choosing is already over," said philosopher and novelist Iris Murdoch.

For us to welcome strangers, the *choosing is already over* in deciding to nurture (or not) the practical, mystical exchange we talked about earlier: recognizing Jesus in immigrants and refugees and being recognized as Jesus by them.

Benedictine monks explicitly try to recognize Jesus in the stranger to whom they offer hospitality. But this isn't all. They're also doing the hard work of Christian formation because they want the stranger to recognize Jesus in them.

I first read *The Rule of Saint Benedict* twenty years ago. After the words, "Let all guests who arrive be received like Christ," it gives instructions for the mystical exchange that Jesus talked about, which include this: "[In] addressing a guest on arrival or departure ... [by] a bow of the head or by a complete prostration of the body, Christ is to be adored because he is indeed welcomed in them."

Once when I visited a Benedictine monastery for lunch, I found it moving when the "Abbot shall pour water [for washing] on the hands of the guests." As he poured the water from a pitcher over my hands, which I held over a bowl, the simple action helped us recognize that something special was happening between us. *The Rule* also reminds us that treating strangers as holy visitors shouldn't be primarily for guests who we would honor anyway—friends, the wealthy, the powerful, those who could help us: "Great care and concern are to be shown in receiving *poor people and pilgrims*, because in them more particularly Christ is received."

This is thoughtful preparation—*the business of choosing that is already over*—for the times when someone sits next to us on the plane, or comes as a guest, or needs help, or applies to cross the border, or when we vote. It doesn't magically transform people into good guests (I'm sure the monks have received plenty of whiny, ungrateful, demanding ones over the centuries) or perfect hosts (I'm sure there have been plenty of gruff and grumpy monks along the way), but it holds up the best possibility that by grace Christ may be seen in the monks by the strangers who are visiting them.

With my children, whose lives I'm shaping more than anyone else's, I want to give them experiences in compassion and model it for them. I want them guided by love and seeing the image of God in everyone. But I also had this conversation again with them recently as we were driving home from school because I'd seen just seen an awful headline about a missing girl:

"So if a stranger comes up and offers you a ride . . ."

"Daaaad . . ."

"But what do you . . ."

"We're going to get in and ask them to take us for ice cream because you won't."

"Seriously."

"Okay, we won't get in . . . if you take us for ice cream now."

Yes, the conversation veered off track quickly because they've heard it before. From the time they were babies, part of my role is helping them navigate interactions with new people. As babies, they went through stages of both naively smiling at anyone who held them and wailing unless in the certain safety of Mom or Dad's arms.

Neither of those (naiveté or tribal clinging) is a good option when we're older. We learn to treat strangers well and with caution. We address serious concerns, as we'll do in the next chapter, not pretend they don't exist. We don't use the word "stranger" much when we get older either. It's more like immigrant, undocumented worker, refugee, foreigner, Muslim, hyphenated-American (not that these should be "strangers," just that they're often treated that way). It takes practice to be both kind and appropriately cautious in the world, with generosity but without climbing into the car with a stranger. It's why our nation has long had in place a vigorous vetting process for refugees to prevent dangerous people from getting in.

Love is the lens we see through, then wisdom guides us through the risks.

Grace is the lens we see through, then the law manages complex reality.

Being fellow children of God is the lens we see through, then we deal with the pluses and minuses of being part of tribes and nations.

Laura recognized the opportunity to pray for and offer her hand on the plane to welcome and comfort the basketball player's fears. After they landed, taxiing along the tarmac, they released hands and started talking. Laura found out the player was getting ready to graduate and look for a job. Laura offered to mentor her. They recognized each other. Welcoming opened the door for new possibilities to help and learn from each other.

Our calling includes welcoming immigrants and refugees as Christ, and praying and practicing welcoming actions so the stranger will see Christ in us.

PRACTICE

Move Along the Good Samaritan Scale

For this practice, choose three steps you can take along the Good Samaritan Scale, which may also involve stepping off of the Slippery Slope Scale.

Here are examples:

- Read a long story about an immigrant or refugee today and let their experience get into your heart and head.

- Have a conversation with someone you are acquainted with who is new to your country. Ask about their experience coming to this country. What has been hardest about leaving home? What has been good and difficult about making this their new home? It's important to do this with care and respect, realizing that trust (for good reason) may need to be built first. If they're willing to share, then listen well.

- Contact a local group or church that works with refugees or immigrants and ask if there's a way you can help.

So what are three simple but specific ways you can move along the scale of recognizing and hoping to be recognized?

REAL
CONCERNS

Where there is love and wisdom, there
is neither fear nor ignorance.

FRANCIS OF ASSISI

When Megan's family moved to New Jersey, her parents called the local public school to register her for kindergarten. She had a severe physical disability. The principal and his team visited and said they wanted to receive her, but just didn't think they could provide the extensive care Megan would need.

Her parents insisted that she thrived around kids and other people. Could he please try?

The principal eventually agreed. He asked her dad to come in and explain to the other kindergarten parents what Pompe disease was, a severe neuromuscular disease that was often fatal (Megan likely wouldn't live through the next year) but wasn't contagious.

She had a wonderful year with the teachers and students. Her dad was making progress on researching medication that helped her gain some strength.

At kindergarten graduation, Megan got extra applause. After the ceremony was over, the principal asked if he could talk with Megan's dad.

"Megan had a great year," said the principal.

"Yes, thank you so much. What you did was remarkable," said the dad.

The principal continued. "I want to share something with you. Right after you gave that talk [before school started] eight months ago, I got a lot of phone calls and letters and emails from those parents. And the message was all the same. It was basically: beautiful young lady, we feel so sorry for her, but boy, kindergarten is such an important year and my son or my daughter won't be able to learn in that environment. Could you please not put my child in that girl's class?"

The dad's feelings were hurt. Why was the principal telling him this? He felt sad for his daughter.

"And I tell you this for a reason," said the principal. "In the last few weeks I've gotten an awful lot of letters and calls and emails. And the message is all consistent, all the same: 'We know this is difficult and it's hard to ask, but our son or our daughter learned so much and had such a great time with Megan in kindergarten. If there's any way that they could be in her first-grade class, we'd owe you the world.'"

I listened to this story while driving. My own dad eyes were teary and my throat constricted as this other dad shared his experience. I paused the podcast to not rush past the moment. I could identify with everyone I'd just heard about. Do you identify with anyone in this story?

I'm the parents of the other kids at the beginning of kindergarten. Of course I hope the girl gets the care she needs and deserves, but I'm so focused on getting what's best for *mine*.

I'm the principal who has every intention to help but initially responds, "No, sorry, it would just take too much effort."

I'm Megan's dad. That could be my daughter in that situation. I feel vulnerable at the thought of being in his shoes, hearing those hurtful words of other parents about her—as though she doesn't have enough challenges. (The entire story is remarkable. Megan's dad founded a biotech company that raced to find medication to keep her and others with Pompe disease alive.)

I'm the different kids as I imagine them in Megan's class at first: the ones who are shy and don't reach out to her, the ones who look on her askew in some way, and then hopefully, in my best moments, the kids who are welcoming and treat her as belonging, as a friend.

Although of course to no extent like Megan in her challenges or her courage, *I too can feel like* I don't fit in, feeling awkward and lonely and needing someone to welcome me. I would guess she has these feelings sometimes.

The borders between us can be physical ability, nationality, ethnicity, sexuality, beliefs, income, and more. We're vulnerable to ignoring, fearing, or even being hostile to people across these borders, which isolates them and can deform us.

Yet crossing the various borders that otherwise keep us apart from our neighbors will, as the parents said to the principal at the end of the kindergarten year, "mean the world to us."

REAL QUESTIONS AND CONCERNS

Immigrants and refugees are by definition crossing national borders to come to us. When we move toward them, we have to cross our own kinds of borders to genuinely welcome them. So naming our concerns is an exercise of hope because our fears can be disarmed as we prepare to connect.

"It strikes me that if what [the advocates for refugees are] trying to do is ever going to work," wrote a journalist who has investigated this concept extensively, "it will depend not on the purity or suffering of the migrants—where the media has chosen to rest its sights—but on the beliefs, prejudices, and fears of their hosts."

Yes it's about *them*, but as dismaying as this is, we do well to admit that it is actually also about *us* and whether we're generous enough for our story to include them. Initially we want to turn away from this reaction that seems self-centered and might feel like taking an Instagram selfie using refugees as a backdrop. But then we can realize that the feeling of discomfort arises because their lives depend on our story, our beliefs, our prejudices, and our fears.

James Baldwin touched on how these kinds of issues are internal (*about us*), not external problems (*about them*) when he wrote about segregation in the United States: "White people will have quite enough to do in learning how to accept and love themselves and each other, and when they have achieved this . . . the Negro problem will no longer exist." This isn't an exact parallel. But as Baldwin was saying that segregation was not an African American or black problem, it was actually a white problem, then in a similar way we can say that this isn't a refugee and immigrant problem (*them*), this is an opportunity to decide how welcoming *we* are.

When I was in Uganda recently I ate lunch with Isaac Anguyo, a seventy-one-year-old northern Ugandan who is a community leader and church elder. He wore a green, yellow, and cream suit that reminded me of Nelson Mandela. His hair is graying but his sense of humor is not; he's quick with a joke. On the other side of me in dark casual dress clothes sat Bishop Alapayo, a fifty-seven-year-old South Sudanese archbishop with responsibility for 1,200 churches in South Sudan.

Isaac talked about how it's fair that Americans have some fear because it's true that some people hate them. But then he said most Muslims are not to be feared. You have to be wise, but still welcome your Muslim sisters and brothers.

"If your life is comfortable, then maybe it's hard to receive all these refugees who come," says Isaac about the South Sudanese coming to his area—more refugees last year than to any other place in the world. "But for us, we had to flee to Sudan before, in the 1980s. We were helped. And so we're ready to help them when they come to us."

They compared experiences on different sides of the border. Bishop Alapayo talked about the destruction and fighting in South Sudan. Isaac talked about his church taking up an offering for the refugees, and how the people in the church, themselves living on minimal resources, brought their own clothes to share.

"How do you find hope?" I mutter, kind of to them, kind of to myself, kind of to God.

"Because other people come to be with us," says Bishop Alapayo. "Only because we're not alone can we find hope."

Be not afraid, that common phrase in Scripture, is a guide for how we welcome. But that doesn't mean we ignore our concerns. We confess them honestly. We see if they're rooted in worrisome fact or in false fear. We seek the truth about what we should and shouldn't do, about how we can welcome without being naive or risking an inordinate cost. Love guides us to be both welcoming and prudent.

Here are some of the concerns about refugees and immigrants that surface most often.

"They'll take our jobs." When we don't feel like we have enough to take care of our loved ones and ourselves, it's hard to provide for someone else. If you don't have a good job, or if you have a good job that could be taken away, how can you be in favor of letting in someone else who is also going to need a job—and might be willing to work for less?

The good news economically is that refugees and immigrants contribute significantly to our economy. On a national scale over the past decade, refugees brought in $63 billion more in government revenues than they cost. On average, refugees are paying more in taxes than they receive in government services and benefits by their ninth year in the country. Multiple studies show that an influx of immigrants or refugees actually helps to raise wages for the local community—not take jobs away. Sometimes at the bottom end of the labor market, wages drop temporarily for less skilled jobs. But then these workers help the economy in the long run by starting small businesses and enabling natives to move into more skilled jobs. Finally, having a younger work force of refugees and immigrants helps a country with an aging population to keep growing economically and to meet promises like Social Security. We shouldn't help primarily so that we ourselves benefit, but care for others often does bring various benefits.

There can be exceptions, and though statistically small, statistics don't change how very hard it is for anyone who loses a job or has to move. So the data is encouraging in the long term, and overall, the fear that "they'll take our jobs" is false. Our generosity in welcoming is rewarded. But we don't want to rush past the fact that on an individual, family, or community level, sometimes there can be a cost to meeting their needs. It takes deep courage, maybe something like a miracle, to be working a hard job, barely making ends meet, and to lift up your eyes to welcome and help someone else in even worse shape.

Yes, people do it. Later in the book you'll meet people like Joseph and Abari Koyomi, refugees in dire situations struggling to support their own children, who then also took on responsibility to foster refugee orphans. But when it's not someone right in front of you, it's harder to give to what can seem distant and abstract when you viscerally face your own family and community needs.

For an American in the US, there is a 1 in 3.64 *billion* chance per year of being murdered by a refugee in a terrorist attack. And there is a 1 in 10.9 *billion* chance of being murdered in a terrorist attack committed by an illegal immigrant. By contrast, there is a lifetime 1 in 7 chance of dying of cancer, a 1 in 303 chance of dying in a car accident, and a 1 in 14,000 chance of being murdered by anyone.

We care because their needs really are worse, since their lives often are in some kind of danger. We care because we're connected as God's children, and loving refugees and immigrants is a way to participate in divine love and meaning for our lives. We can also care without being overwhelmed by worry that immigrants will take our jobs. Biblical hospitality can, in the long term, lead to a greater harvest, shared by many.

"We'll be risking crime and our security." When I'm at the beach, my visceral fear of sharks can influence my choices more than worry about skin cancer, even though statistically the sun's rays are much more dangerous to me.

We do well to honestly admit that unreasonable, dramatic fear can have power over us. With a rigorous vetting system that has long been in place, there are very few risks to welcoming refugees. No American citizen has lost their life in a terrorist attack perpetrated by a refugee since the Refugee Act was passed in 1980. In the Boston Marathon bombing, the Orlando Pulse nightclub shooting, 9/11, and others, the perpetrators of other ethnicities get lumped in with the refugee risk, though none of these perpetrators were refugees. (Incidentally, white men commit the majority of mass shootings in our country.) Undocumented workers have murdered people in our country; millions live here. But studies seem to show that the presence of more immigrants in a neighborhood makes it statistically safer.

The vetting process for refugees is extremely rigorous and goes through multiple interviews, background checks, and review by Homeland Security.

Around the same time period that Dylan Roof murdered nine people in an African American church in Charleston, we had awful elementary school shootings and other similar attacks. Any violent events that appear related to immigrants and refugees can work on the public imagination like shark attacks, stoking fear in the majority culture. Actually, the likelihood of being attacked by a shark (1 in 3,748,067) or by lightning (1 in 79,749) or heart disease (1 in 5) are much, much higher than the odds of being an American killed by a refugee terrorist attack (1 in 3.64 billion).

"There is evidence showing that when a small number of native workers are displaced by new migrants entering the workforce, those native workers end up in higher-paying, higher-skill jobs. . . .

"In two instances the arrival of migrants had either no effect or a positive effect on the local labor market:

- "The arrival of 125,000 Cubans into Miami [in 1980] had no effect on unemployment and was followed by a small rise in average low-skill wages.
- "And the movement of Soviet refugees into Israel [in the 1990s], enough to raise the country's population 12 percent in just four years, saw a substantial rise in the wages of the occupations they crowded into."

But even if the risks are small with refugees, because of all the other reasonable fears in life, why not cut out *any* risk over which we have relatively easy (border) control?

The answer, which we looked at in earlier chapters, is that we want love instead of fear to animate our lives. Otherwise we fall prey to the bigger risk: we lose part of our own humanity if we don't respond to people in need. But with small, wise risks we can give an incredible opportunity to the refugees and immigrants we help.

"There is no fear in love, but perfect love casts out fear" (1 John 4:18). I've experienced how loving outwardly can help chase away my inward worry. This Bible passage talks about God's love casting out our need for fear—because God loves us. Thinking of refugees, the verse also points toward how loving other people can help cast fear out of *their* lives. When we help a family out of the bombings and chemical attacks of Syria, then we help to chase away *their* fear so that love takes its place.

"God is love, and those who *abide* in love *abide* in God, and God *abides* in them," comes soon after that verse in 1 John, with that emphasized word *abide* used three times. This sentence speaks of the kind of home we want for ourselves and others. This is about where we truly belong: love is our only true home. Part of how we love is by helping others to abide in God's love and to abide in homes where they can be safe.

"We need to focus on taking care of our own." We are tribal. This isn't a sin or a fault. It's how people function. The benefit comes because being connected *in* relationships makes life fuller and safer, but the danger lies in how we treat and think of people as *out*.

Sebastian Junger, known for his book *The Perfect Storm* and his wartime journalism, recently wrote a book called *Tribe: On Homecoming and Belonging*. Reading it while considering refugees and immigrants, I was struck toward the end: "Belonging to society requires sacrifice, and that sacrifice gives back way more than it costs. . . . That sense of solidarity is at the core of what it means to be human."

Our challenge is to find the solidarity that we need by belonging to *tribes* in our communities, churches, and nations, while also welcoming others who have, as immigrants or refugees, been forced to flee their own tribes and are now disconnected. We need to protect and nurture the benefits of belonging while also welcoming people who need to belong. Despite—and, actually, because of—the pain caused by our nation's history (when people's tribal land was taken from them and others were taken from their tribes in Africa into slavery), we can also take a stand for ideals (democracy, the suffrage movement, Civil Rights) of diverse people being able to come together as a tribe to live as fellow citizens and help each other as neighbors.

The first chapter told of John Dutcher saying that he hated Muslims. They weren't part of his tribe. Then Muslim families moved into his apartment. Together they became, effectively, part of an apartment tribe, looking out for each other and belonging together.

We can enjoy being part of tribes. But we need to be even more deeply grounded in belonging to God's family, which means welcoming those displaced from their tribes.

"They're changing our town." As Christians we should love diversity because God's kingdom is diverse, with people of every kind. In the book of Revelation we see "a great multitude that no one could count, from every nation, from all tribes and peoples and languages, standing before the throne and before the Lamb" (7:9).

That is the ultimate guiding vision of God's kingdom, whose beauty we should embrace as part of this discussion of refugees and immigrants. Yet we can also see, as we did earlier, that there is strength in the tribe. God chose Israel in a special way. He literally chose tribes and instructed them on protecting their tribe-ness. My experience is *diverse* = better, but it isn't the only formula of faithful, good living. Urbanites with lots of diversity around them probably do well to confess that they can be condescending to others who aren't in cities or churches as diverse as their own.

At the same time, change makes many of us feel vulnerable. People from different places bring goodness, but their influence can also take away goodness that was there before.

Dina Nayeri fled Iran as a child and came to the US as a refugee. Years later she wrote a sharp-edged essay about responding to people in extreme need: "Even if the country gets overcrowded and you have to give up your luxuries, and we set up ugly little lives around the corner, marring your view. If we need a lot of help and local services, if your taxes rise and your street begins to look and feel strange and everything smells like turmeric and tamarind paste, and your favourite shop is replaced by a halal butcher, your schoolyard chatter becoming ching-chongese and phlegmy 'kh's and 'gh's'"—even so, we still simply owe them "a basic human obligation. It is the obligation of every person born in a safer room to open the door when someone in danger knocks."

Her provocation doesn't hide that people are losing a lot—that there is a cost in the change. She just doesn't feel sorry about the cost because the people they've welcomed had to flee their home and lost so much more. She believes, as we should, that it is worth the discomfort of change to accept the responsibility as a "person born in a safer room to open the door when someone in danger knocks."

I saw an Associated Press report about change like this in Androscoggin County, Maine, which has accepted 7,500 African refugees since 2001 into a county of just over 100,000 people. That creates a lot of demographic change for the residents to wrestle with.

The loss of lifestyle that comes with change—different tribes instead of the one you felt comfortable with, different languages, changing jobs—can be honored. But for those who experience fear or loss, confession can help us meet this change with lament instead of anger. Change is the price of a love that welcomes. Jesus' vision of loving our neighbors should keep nostalgia from calcifying into a bitter vision for recapturing old, whitewashed days. Part of what can be hard is that you had no say in, for example, the government's local resettlement policy. Anger at what is lost can lead us to lash out at those bringing the change, but mourning the loss can open us to the beauty of discovering what is next.

We don't know exactly what that "next" will be, but we can step into the change knowing we're participating in God's love: "[God] defends the cause of the fatherless and the widow, and loves the foreigner residing among you, giving them food and clothing. And you are to love those who are foreigners, for you yourselves were foreigners in Egypt" (Deuteronomy 10:18-19 NIV).

We can hope that even if the change is bumpy, as Nayeri's sarcasm shows, what lies on the other side usually isn't our worst fear. Instead, we actually find a beauty that takes some effort but that also takes us closer to God's kingdom in which every tribe and nation and language lives and worships together.

"We're letting too many people in." "I often think of America as a lifeboat and a lot of the world is a raging ocean," said TV show host Bill Maher. "Everybody wants to get in the lifeboat. And certainly everybody has a right to be happy in the world. But if too many people get in the lifeboat, then the lifeboat goes down. We want to rescue people who are drowning. But eventually if you let too many people in, we'll sink."

No, not everybody wants to come to America, but Maher's comment gets to the point that it's more complicated than opening our arms wide and saying, "Let everyone in who wants to come!"

My cousin John Stackhouse, a professor in Canada, sees parallels for North Americans in how God instructed Israel to care for the stranger but also to protect its borders. We should welcome, he says, but "societies also correctly maintain their integrity by being careful how much 'difference' they introduce into their social bloodstream, how much change they try to accommodate."

"We, too," he says, "should use our wealth and power to care for the needy. But we also should use our heads and not compromise precisely what makes Canada so attractive to so many people around the world . . . our democracy, respect for law, stable institutions, social safety net, and, indeed, our regard and accommodation for differences in our neighbors even as we help them assimilate into our common life."

The United States should welcome more generously. For example, in response to the Vietnam War, we welcomed 800,000 Vietnamese. Compare that to this moment of global refugee crisis, when we're cutting back by about 75 percent how many we welcome each year. At the same time, as Stackhouse warns, different sides in the debate can oversimplify: "No few Bible verses . . . can provide a shortcut past the difficult conversation we have been having, and must continue to have, about immigration policy in this country."

We should welcome more refugees, but we also have to continue the same kind of vetting that has ensured that no American life has been taken by a refugee in a terrorist act since the Refugee Act of 1980—and some number of refugees does have to be decided on. With immigrants, our society has to choose how many to welcome and how to create a fair, dignified system. Europe has demonstrated generosity toward refugees, while also showing some problems of failed integration. Surely we have a moral duty not to deport those who were brought here as children, those who are in school or have graduated, worked hard, complied with laws, paid taxes, and been good neighbors.

Yes, there should be wise limits. We should be more generous in helping other nations receive their neighbors. Experts emphasize how important refugee care is in countries next to violent conflict or drought that causes people to flee. These countries receive so many more refugees. We will never bring most of the refugees to our country, and that's not the best-case scenario. These are all complex issues that need to be wrestled with and decided.

Immigrants and refugees both challenge and affirm the narrative of America. The United States has been a place of refuge and opportunity for many strangers (as seen in immigrant American dream stories), a place of refusal for others (during travel bans), a place of purgatory for millions (particularly undocumented workers), and a place of exploitative oppression past and present for still others (including Native Americans, slaves, and their descendants).

This isn't a political statement. This is being honest people who love our neighbors and respect the cloud of witnesses who have gone before us. Welcoming refugees and immigrants gives us a chance to live toward Statue of Liberty ideals.

Finally, with the annual refugee cap now at its lowest by far since Ronald Reagan who one year set the cap at 140,000, we certainly can welcome more. There is a limit somewhere, but unemployment is very low even after we have been welcoming about 100,000 people a year. We receive only 0.2 percent of the world's refugees. Our nation has proven that we can handle it economically (to the country's benefit), the process is safe (see the security statistics above), and those who live in diverse neighborhoods benefit economically in a neighborhood that looks more like the residents of God's kingdom.

We aren't called to first defend our country's borders or honor, but to seek the kingdom of God. We seek comfort, patriotism, war, power, pleasure, success, and so many other things first. We seek liberal, libertarian, or conservative stairways to heaven rather than going down on our knees to love, learn, and pray. We don't want to huddle within bonds of racism or nationalism, but instead to cross borders into the liberation of God's kingdom.

"We're already too busy and overwhelmed." A psychological study in 1972 was done at Princeton Seminary, and I feel lucky that it was done long before I was a student on campus because I can't be sure what I would have done.

Students were set up to preach on Jesus' story of the Good Samaritan. Then they had to walk across campus to deliver the talk they'd prepared. The psychologists did two things. First, they gave students one of three different time pressures: no rush, better get right over, or hurry up because you're late. Second, they put an actor along the way "sitting slumped in a doorway, head down, eyes closed, not moving." Someone like the man in Jesus' story who had been robbed and needed help.

The subject matter of what they were giving a talk on didn't make much difference for whether the students stopped to help the man. In other words, students preparing to talk on the Good Samaritan did not stop more or less than the control group that had a different topic.

But results varied dramatically for those who were or weren't in a hurry. In low-hurry situations, 63 percent stopped to help. Students who felt especially pressed for time stopped to help only 10 percent of the time.

The pressures in our lives make a difference for whether we respond compassionately. We're prone to not loving our neighbors, even those who are suffering the most, when we're hurried or stressed. If we don't pause, we can miss or underestimate people's suffering, whether they are immigrants, refugees, or someone on the sidewalk on our way to work. Paying attention, we can hear love whisper, *There is your neighbor*, and then we can follow toward meaningful encounters, like the Good Samaritan and the beat-up man lying by the side of the road. If we watch for God, Jesus says that in these moments we find God in each other.

We also do well to confess that if we're able to rush past someone who is at the very nadir of life, then we're likely in a position of some degree of privilege.

Once after a trip to Haiti I landed in Miami around 9:00 p.m. Waited in line. Passport checked. Cleared. I was walking down that final customs hallway before I'd catch a shuttle, get my car, and drive two hours home.

Tired after an intense trip, I was eager to go the last thirty feet past the final customs officer when he started berating an older man who was behind me.

The older man didn't appear to understand English. It may have been his first time to the United States. The power differential between a customs official and a visitor to our country, in that moment, is close to absolute. He's totally at their mercy. Usually agents are professional and courteous, but not this one.

Rather than stepping in and saying to the disrespectful official, "Excuse me, sir, can you be kinder?" or asking, "Is there any way I could help the man?" instead of being the one person who could have turned that moment from darkness toward light, I just kept walking.

I was not tired enough to justify this moment of willful deafness. Was there a 15 percent chance I would have annoyed the customs officer and been delayed? A .001 percent chance of a strip search? Whatever the risk, I shouldn't have cared.

Privilege demands a price. In this case it cost this elderly man abuse. It cost the immigration officer some piece of his soul to treat someone in that degrading way. And me? The cost was that I floated through without love, and without risk. My soul became even more calloused as I received dignified treatment I didn't earn or deserve, because if any of the three of us deserved special respect, it was the old man.

My last book included a few pages about confessing privilege, and often this was the section that made readers balk. After my lectures, over coffee, or via email, I talked with some people who liked the practices and vision in my book. But they wondered if "confessing privilege" was code for liberal politics. Many of these people were faithful, white, working-class people who also struggled with serious physical disabilities, job loss, and addictions. "Privilege" did not characterize how they felt they were experiencing life's struggle, which I understood.

But my experiences—in Haiti, and both in good ways and in shameful ways as in that airport—have taught me how confessing privilege shouldn't be thought of as loss or as guilt manipulation by identity politics. No, confessing privilege actually provides a way we can all gain. As someone who is white, middle-class, educated, et cetera, living in Haiti helped me understand more deeply the pain of US history and systems, and it showed me how I couldn't ignore them. It helped me learn about power dynamics that we have to understand if we're going to work well together for justice. Confessing privilege, to whatever extent we have it, helps us to be more welcoming because we cultivate gratitude, our hearts stay sensitive to the situations of others, and we can slow down to better see how to help. Confessing privilege makes us vulnerable in a good way, and we miss out on so much good change (for others and ourselves) if we don't.

Confessing privilege and being aware of how stress and busy-ness make us rush past the needs of others can help us take steps to listen to that whisper of God and help our neighbor.

"We're not sure what God is doing about all of this." This is probably thought more than said out loud.

Slowing down to recognize the suffering that so many immigrants and refugees face makes my faith feel vulnerable at times. This is a confession of the psalms.

The scene from Elie Weisel's *Night* comes to mind, an incident when three men were hung in the prison camp during the World War II Holocaust. Weisel and the other prisoners were marched past and saw that two of them were already dead. The third was still barely alive, with his tongue "still red, his eyes not yet extinguished." Wiesel writes,

Behind me, I heard the same man asking:

"For God's sake, where is God?"

And from within me, I heard a voice answer:

"Where He is? This is where—hanging here from this gallows."

We see the suffering of God's people and cry with the psalmists, "How long, Oh Lord?" I plead about God's inaction. Yet I also see that God is in the suffering.

I wrote about faith, doubt, and suffering in my book *After Shock*. One idea in the book that resonated with many readers is that with each crisis of faith, what we believe is crucified. Then we wait expectantly, whether despairing or hopeful, to see what part of our faith is resurrected.

Looking seriously at the plight of these refugees and immigrants should cause some kind of crisis of faith. Maybe that's why we look away—to avoid seeing crucifixion. We're aware that for many this experience is a road that leads to suffering and then to death. We don't pretend otherwise. I feel bruised spending a year on this topic—and I'm not even close to living it.

So look and listen carefully and honestly, humbly and prayerfully, seeking God. And then, yes, as the psalms almost always turn in the end to praise and gratitude, we will also get to see courage, kindness, and even resurrection.

CAN WE RISK HOPE?

Our hope is strong enough to overcome the fears and vulnerabilities we've just looked at—this hope that love will heal, welcome, and transform the world and our lives.

Megan, who has Pompe disease, continued into first grade and through to high school graduation. Then it was time for college.

"Megan is the most physically challenged student to go to University of Notre Dame," her dad explained. "She's the only student to have to live in a wheelchair, on a ventilator, with 24/7 nursing."

The university made lots of accommodations to make it possible for Megan to attend—ensuring classrooms were accessible, making sure her dorm room would work for her needs.

"Where I was most proud," continued her dad, "was one thing we hadn't thought about: Megan is a twenty-year-old young lady now who weighs about 120 pounds. While you only need one nurse there to care for her, it takes two people to transfer her in and out of her wheelchair. I hadn't thought of who that second person was going to be. When I was in her dorm room that second weekend, . . . I saw the nursing schedule on the board. And then I saw a schedule next to it. It was students who had signed up in her dorm to be there seven times a day, at specific times, to get [Megan] in and out of her wheelchair."

You welcomed me, Megan can say to them, as physical borders that would have kept Megan from classes opened up. The university students, like the students in Megan's kindergarten class, surely also feel like they were welcomed by Megan into a new, more tender and meaningful way to be alive. They show us a hopeful scene of how borders can be crossed by love that commits to daily hard work.

Are we going to be transformed through welcoming, like Megan's kindergarten classmates were? Are we going to sign up like her dormmates to help her get in and out of her wheelchair?

When we do this—abide in love, as love abides in us—we're able to cross over each concern we just looked at:

You helped me even though you were concerned about your job and providing for your own family.

You took some risk to receive me but not foolish risk.

You reached beyond your tribe to help me belong.

You faced the discomfort of change that I bring and sought the beauty in my presence.

You opened the door to welcome as many of the people in situations like mine as you could.

You slowed down to recognize me and recognize your privilege instead of walking past; then you could help and we could find something more meaningful together.

You looked for God in my suffering and my healing.

You chose again and again to welcome hope and to welcome me.

PRACTICE

Connect with Neighbors Across Borders

How can we find freedom into welcoming across these concerns, across these borders? In this practice we'll consider them first for ourselves, then for someone else. The idea is to step toward any fears about immigrants and refugees—and then seek how God's love illuminates.

The first part of this practice is to ask whether you feel any of the concerns in this chapter. Which ones? Why? It could be that you didn't have some of this information, or that you hadn't thought of it in this way. Maybe you still need more information by reading, researching, or talking with people. It could be an uncomfortable reaction you feel in yourself about people of other ethnicities. Or maybe you're just not quite sure about one of the concerns and need time to think. Take a few minutes to flip back through the concerns in this chapter to see what makes you uncomfortable.

The God who first loved us and welcomes us wants us to care for others who are vulnerable and foreigners, so we want to confess these concerns honestly and seriously. And then we see whether our fears may be confirmed, altered, or chased out by truth and love. (If you don't have any concerns, first be sure that's true, then you can move to the second part of this practice.)

Now the second part of this practice is to pick a concern or two in this chapter that you have heard from someone else that you want to consider together. Think about someone you could communicate with about the concerns. You're doing this to understand them and hopefully gain clarity together, not to judge them.

Have a conversation about one or more of these concerns that is flowing with grace—whatever preparation that takes. On this issue (like other political issues) sometimes the border that needs crossing consists of having conversations like this with people in your church, community, or even family. You could bring it up in conversation, invite them to read this chapter, or find some other way to enter into discussion. Don't approach it by judging them, but instead by confessing first your own fears and concerns. Pray that new discoveries will be made together.

Either of these steps may lead to some kind of practical action: to do more research, to visit a local nonprofit that works with refugees, to find an expert to talk with. This chapter focuses on confessing and addressing our concerns, but we always want to be open to the Spirit prompting us toward action.

THIS IS
OUR STORY

*Stories can conquer fear, you know. They
can make the heart bigger.*

Ben Okri

*T*he old man in a gray suit sits in the front row. He
looks about eighty years old. The seating climbs up
behind him like rows in a movie theater. Every seat is full.

"Is there anyone in our audience tonight who owes their
life to Nicholas Winton?" says the BBC announcer. "If so,
could you stand up please."

Winton is invited to stand. He turns around. He sees
them all standing.

"On behalf of all of them, thank you very much indeed,"
says the announcer.

They all sit back down. Winton rubs tears from under
his glasses.

For about fifty years these children, who are now older
adults, had not known who saved them. Winton apparently

did not tell anyone what he had done as a young man in Britain, a stockbroker, watching Nazi horrors unfold from a distance in Czechoslovakia in 1939 just before World War II.

He decided to try to understand the situation better and see if he could help. He visited the Czech camps where mostly Jewish people were imprisoned.

"Immigration wasn't an option," says a *60 Minutes* report about Winton's life. "The world's doors were closed to the refugees. Conditions in the camps were brutal for the 150,000 people trapped there, especially for the children."

Winton went to meet the families. He came back and worked through the bureaucracy, forging or lying when necessary, so these children could take a train across the heart of Nazi Germany to Britain to be adopted—so they could escape the camps, and probable death, and be welcomed into new lives.

Winton saved 669 children who would have died otherwise. They, their children, and their grandchildren were sitting and then standing around him in that theater.

Only toward the end of his life did he get to hear the stories he made possible. Their stories made his own story incredible.

A middle-aged woman in a purple suit shows the border pass that she received because of his efforts, which she wore around her neck as a child. "I'm another of the children you saved," she says, and gives him a kiss on the cheek.

It's almost too much to take all at once: the story of evil and suffering being thwarted by generosity and kindness, then remembered with this simple, tender kiss. You're scrolling through Facebook and without warning, right after a cat does something cute and silly, a video takes you to the heart of a beautiful, meaningful life.

When we welcome, new stories are made. And to welcome well, like Winton, we need to pay attention and listen deeply to people's lives so we can see how best to help and where it will lead our own story.

HOW THESE STORIES ARE AND AREN'T ABOUT US

In the last chapter, we confessed the importance of addressing our concerns so we can respond well to immigrants and refugees. Winton's story continues to lead us farther in that direction.

What kind of story do you want your life to tell?

But wait, it's kind of disgusting, isn't it, that even this becomes about us? We're appalled when that friend or acquaintance, leader or celebrity makes everything about *themselves*. There's a tsunami that kills 100,000 people—and somehow that becomes about how *my* experience was so harrowing as *I* was witnessing their suffering.

The refugee and immigrant stories are in many ways about *you*. And about *me*. But this isn't license for self-absorption. Quite the opposite. Because of the vulnerable situation they're forced into—of needing some place and some people to receive them—this is about those of *us* who aren't refugees and immigrants, much more than we'd like. This is an invitation to change our story by respecting them deeply and listening closely and becoming part of their stories. That's what Winton did. That's how his story became extraordinary.

The journalist who said in the last chapter that it is about *us* is partly right when he says, "I'm not sure it's possible to tell any of these [refugee] stories plainly, with open heart and without agenda. . . . Everyone I talk to seems to have already made a decision about the 'refugee question': whether to open borders completely . . . or close them to the masses of false refugees, secret terrorists and 'economic migrants' who, according to [some] politicians . . . make up the majority of asylum seekers."

In his fascinating article about a German village of about one hundred people receiving over seven hundred refugees, he adds how these stories come to us in a "trap of condescension: flattening their subjects into simple creatures of suffering and good intention. They want a roof, a job. They love . . . democracy. They suffer nobly."

Jesus told us to love our neighbors as ourselves. This means we cannot flatten refugees or immigrants, even for noble purposes. The journalist goes on, "If it is a dehumanizing lie to suggest that all refugees are criminals . . . it is no less a lie to depict them as hapless victims. My own experiences suggest that refugees are as diverse as any other randomly assembled group of people."

In this chapter, we'll first hear three stories of stepping into the unknown, of being separated, of showing grit, that strike a universal chord. Their stories are like our stories, while also being so very different and worth listening to. Then we'll look at why it matters what stories we're close to, see why it helps to understand our own stories, and reflect on how stories lead to change as we're invited into this story of God's first welcoming us so we can freely welcome others.

INTO THE UNKNOWN—A MAN RISKS HIS LIFE FLEEING WAR BY TRYING TO CROSS THE MEDITERRANEAN SEA

You stand on the shore just before dawn.

A warm breeze blows. A hint of a hint of a hint of light glimmers over the dark expanse of the Mediterranean Sea. You might just be hoping for that. You need a hint of hope. Your tears are gone. The fear envelops you.

Before you the earth seems a formless void. Darkness covers the face of the deep. You're back before creation. This trip will take you either to new creation or down deep forever into the void.

"Come on! Move it! Move it, idiots!"

You have to step into the water toward the small boat. Bodies press all around you. You're being pushed together out into the water. You gave them your life savings, plus a loan, plus your sisters gave all their savings. Your sixty-seven-year-old mother you will probably never see again. She was sending her only beloved son toward a boat, you think, as you slosh forward, trying not to fall. You gave them everything to risk your life. Now they call you "idiot."

You climb in. Arms and legs. Like one tangled flesh of hope and misery and escape and fear, the ninety of you. *Nothing to lose* means you've already lost everything except climbing onto this boat.

You start bouncing through the waves. If you win the lottery, you land on the foreign shore of a country where many people don't want you and you have to start with nothing with nobody without speaking the language and with no place to sleep. Then you have to create a life *ex nihilo*. That's the best case scenario.

You look in all directions and see only water. There is only water. Moses is not raising his wooden staff to part the waves so you can walk to safety through dry land. No land anywhere. You raise your hand. "Please, God," you dare whisper.

Water still everywhere. Waves. You will drift to the bottom, that is all.

You are all covered in seasick vomit. You've all been throwing up onto each other.

Lights flash. You think you're dying. Which may be relief. May be. Then voices squawking. Yelling. You're numb. No fear left. Are you going to be sunk? Or taken back? You feel panic. You're going to throw yourself into the water. Anything but back.

But another boat has pulled up. They're reaching down.

Someone welcomes you into her arms. She puts a towel around you and averts her eyes as you pull off your vomit-stained shirt and pants, your piss-and-diarrhea-stained underwear. Your body barely feels your own. It doesn't feel like any dignity belongs to it still. But this boat now makes you feel like you might still belong on this planet. Your body, your self, might still belong.

So much left behind. So much unknown ahead. But right now, here you are welcomed on this boat. You can imagine that it is going somewhere other than down into the dark-forever abyss.

While not pretending to understand the experience of someone escaping from, say, Gambia in western Africa, eventually to Libya, then to try to cross the sea to Europe, this story of loss is an extreme of something we all feel. In illness, in losing a loved one or a job, in a crisis of doubt, we feel adrift. Though ours can't compare to theirs, to some degree we still recognize *that is me* and *that could be me* at the extreme.

We listen to hear what our stories mean to each other.

RIPPED APART—A DAUGHTER WATCHES HER FATHER TAKEN FROM HER IN OUR OWN COUNTRY

On Tuesday morning as your dad drives you to school, you fuss with your long brown hair. In middle school you'd better have your hair and clothes just right. You always like this drive talking with dad—about friends, about a quiz that day, about running—before school starts.

Recently he helped you train for a marathon. You teased him for not running, but still he was out riding the bike next to you every day: keep going, you can do it! And you did it! You ran the marathon. He was so proud to see you with the big shiny medal around your neck. He's always so proud of you.

Then lights flash on a car behind you. Some kind of police pull you over. They take him away. They take your dad! Handcuffed. Like a criminal. *What did he do? He only helps people! He only works hard! He only loves me!*

"Back to Mexico," you hear one of them say. You were born here. You've never been to Mexico. They can't take him back, can they? But they take him.

You start sobbing. You've never felt so helpless.

After they drive him away, you decide to go to school anyway. Dad always went to work. He always took you to school. He helped you push through when your legs ached and your side cramped so you could be ready for the marathon. You still go to school because you think that's what he would have wanted, but they've ripped your heart away and put him in jail.

The system was broken; the politicians bickered and couldn't come to an agreement. The country was dysfunctional for decades about enticing immigrants with offers to pay them for work, as they paid taxes and contributed to the economy, but didn't give a clear way to make it legal. Your dad followed opportunity to provide for his family. You were a child and didn't do anything wrong. There is a way to fix a system, to require people to go through a fair and legal process, maybe to pay some kind of fair price, and still care about people. Yes, they can still care about you and your having a dad to care for you.

But they chose to pull your car over and take your dad away. You lose your dad. A country loses its heart and integrity and ideals while feigning, in part, to care about legality.

You heard about other stories like this, and now it's your story too. Another even harder marathon begins: to try to push through and find how this story can lead to a happy ending.

GRITTY LOVE—A REFUGEE WELCOMES
THREE ORPHANS WITH OPEN ARMS

Joseph is standing on the red clay of northern Uganda with young children playing near his feet as I listen to his story. He had been a successful doctor, then his country exploded again, and ten months ago to escape with his life, he walked for four days, leaving everything behind to arrive here on this 30 x 30–foot plot in Bidi Bidi Camp with 287,000 others from South Sudan.

He's wearing a brown tank top, dark slacks, and plastic flip-flops. He's sinewy, muscular. He shifts back and forth as he talks. He's intense, with a quick smile. He describes how hard the conditions are here. He mentions he's HIV positive and receives daily meds from the clinic.

Nearby are a tarp tent and a small red brick home about 10 x 7 feet big. He built it. He learned how to make bricks here and has been selling them for extra income. He's farming on his little plot. He has also found a way to farm a small section of land nearby with permission from local Ugandans. At first he planted corn, but cows trampled and ate it.

Can you imagine having to start over in these conditions, again and again and again? He planted sorghum and other crops that made it to harvest.

Oh, and he's a foster parent to three children because, like many children, they came over without parents. Yes, in these fight-for-survival circumstances as a refugee himself caring for his own family, he also welcomed three orphans—not related to him, each from a different tribe than his.

He wants the kids to have variety in their diet and good nutrition, so he works extra hard at farming. He doesn't get paid anything for fostering these children. They only get the children's regular food ration, which everyone says isn't enough.

"I really want to go home," he says, "but only after these children are set up for good."

He picks at the callouses on his hands as he talks.

"These used to be smooth dentist hands," he says. "This is from work here."

They are rough, rough hands, every part jagged with thick callouses.

I think of *Grit*, a popular book a few years ago. The subtitle is *The Power of Passion and Perseverance*. The kind of book middle-class parents (like me) buy to help their children toward success because we're scared they're too soft. I know we're not supposed to flatten refugees with their stories, but I'm standing here talking with *Grit* himself. He's incredible. He has the group of Ugandan visitors around him laughing with him as he describes his failures and successes.

The small group we were visiting with walks away, and I keep talking with him for a few minutes. I ask about his work. I'm in awe of him. I don't want to walk away yet.

He describes going out to the fields, then as an aside says his flip-flops are tough to do that work in, back through the bush.

I think for a second. I have black leather casual dress shoes on. They're good shoes: Josef Sobel; about $120 five years ago; comfortable, flexible sole. Then I make what is not a noble move. It's really an amateur move, the kind I have advised others against. I've given gifts before, but in circumstances like this it's usually best not to. But for whatever reason, I feel like I'm standing on holy ground here with Joseph and these other 286,999 people.

As of the end of 2015, half of the refugees in the world had been in exile for four years or more. And on average, a refugee is in exile for more than ten years.

"Want to trade shoes?"

"Really?"

"Only if you want to. Only if they'd help."

"Let me try."

I lean on his shoulder and untie my shoe. We trade. He puts mine on. Laces them up. Walks around. He tests whether my shoes would work well. He's living too close to the edge to take charity just because it's charity—if it's not going to be an effective tool for survival.

"I think this will be very good. You certain?"

"Would be my honor."

We trade shoes.

"You know," he says, "the Israelites wandered in the desert for a long time, but God then showed them the way home. I want to go home. I really want to go home. But my work now is here."

Joseph and I give a handshake hug. As I walk away, the kids point at my feet and laugh, thinking it's pretty funny that I'm walking away in flip-flops.

As I walk, I'm wondering what happened. Sometimes holy ground makes you do strange things. Maybe selfishly I offered my shoes so I could stay connected with Joseph somehow. Get to keep walking on holy ground. There was nothing special about what I did. I got the better part of the deal, though he got the better farming shoes.

We don't want to flatten Joseph, but we do well to be inspired by his grit in welcoming strangers—these kids from three tribes different than his own. May our own grit, my own grit, in welcoming be even somewhat worthy of his.

Most refugees stay in countries near where they had to flee, and going to resettle in a country like the United States, Canada, or Australia is never a possibility. "In 2016 there were 17.5 million registered refugees. Of this number, the UN Refugee Agency made just 162,500 [that is, less than 1%] eligible for resettlement. These are the extraordinary cases: people with certain medical conditions, victims of torture, or families facing some particular hardship."

THE STORIES WE CHOOSE TO BE CLOSE TO

Who we're close to in many ways determines who we become. I don't know if I'll be able to live well enough to honor briefly walking in Joseph's shoes—literally and through empathy. But I do know something in me changes by being with him.

A study a couple of years ago about evangelical Christian attitudes on immigration looked at what most influenced people's thinking. The responses were (starting with what had the most influence) immigrants they had interacted with, friends and family, the media, the Bible, and then immigrants they had observed. (Everything else was less than 5 percent, including the church, at 2 percent.) The stories of people we're close to made the most difference.

After one of the rallies in this recent public resurgence of white supremacy, a doctor named Esther Choo wrote a series of tweets that got wide circulation. Her experience is both depressing and hopeful:

We've got a lot of white nationalists in Oregon. So a few times a year, a patient in the ER refuses treatment from me because of my race. I don't get angry or upset, just incredulous over the psychology of it.

The conversation usually goes like this:

Me: "I understand your viewpoint. I trained at elite institutions and have been practicing for fifteen years. You are welcome to refuse care under my hands, but I feel confident that I am the most qualified to care for you. Especially since the alternative is an intern."

And they invariably pick the intern—as long as the intern is white. Or they leave. Breathtaking, isn't it? To be so wedded to your theory of white superiority that you will bet your life on it, even in the face of clear evidence to the contrary?

Sometimes I just look at them, my kin in 99.9 percent of our genetic code, and fail to believe they don't see our shared humanity.

This is tragic and not surprising, just jarring when it's so blatant and blinding in a moment like that when the person is going against truth and common humanity at the same time. (I liked how Choo put the "love your neighbor" idea into DNA terms.) Then, fortunately, she says there are sometimes glimpses of light.

You know what gives me hope? A few get uncomfortable and apologize in the same breath they refuse to let me treat them. You see, it's a hell of a hard thing to maintain that level of hate face-to-face.

Proximity can sometimes break through even the hardest of us. This is the kind of fierce revelation (and potential for grace) of a Flannery O'Connor short story, when you realize the doctor who you abstractly hated and thought inferior could now save your life through her brilliance. Choo concludes,

I used to cycle through disbelief, shame, anger. Now I just show compassion and move on. I figure the best thing I can do . . . is make sure their hate finds no purchase here.

An important way we give love more purchase than hate is by choosing who we're near so their stories are shaping us. In whatever ways I'm growing in love (and there are plenty; I have a long way to go), one of the wisest things I've done in my life is to repeatedly choose to be around people who enlarge my understanding of God, who give me perspective on how most people in the world live, and who demonstrate love better than I do. Their stories shape me. I need them. And then—after I meet someone like Joseph—I'm compelled to try to live in a way worthy of the grace that our stories intersected.

THE STORY OF OURSELVES

If we want to be a good part of other people's stories, it helps to understand our own story. When I asked a longtime foreign aid worker in Jordan what he has learned about welcoming refugees in his role for the past year, he told me, "In a way it's just like welcoming someone in the US or Canada, giving someone hospitality. You want to understand where they're coming from—and also be self-aware of your own preconceptions so they don't get in the way and you're freed to understand the issues more deeply."

In Haiti where I've worked, living there and visiting regularly for fifteen years, it's important to understand the context of colonization, exploitation, liberation, leadership, missions, foreign aid, and independence. If you were to work on a Native American reservation, presumably you'd better know something about the history of the tribe and also find a way to submit to Native American leadership in what you do. Like the doctor's oath "First, do no harm," self-understanding can help keep us from doing harm—and hopefully also help free us into serving well.

Most of us in America are the children of immigrants. I've been learning recently from friends like Lisa Sharon Harper, who is a leader on justice issues including racial reconciliation, about how the category "white" has been used to differentiate people groups and often protect the power of those who fit this (sometimes changing) category and to exclude and exploit those outside. In addition to the other harm this has done, the category separates those of us who are "white" from our roots.

"It's not too late to reroot self in what's real: ethnic heritage(s), family story and DNA," instead of in the false construct of being "white" when everyone else is "from somewhere," Harper said recently. That is, instead of understanding my identity as "white," it's healthy to know my family's history, including our own immigration story and ways that our ancestors were part of exploiting and/or being exploited, as well as the courage and grit it usually took to make a new life.

When the Irish came over to escape the potato famine, they were disparaged and discriminated against. Eastern Europeans were later looked down on as they immigrated. Recently I was talking with a friend of Chinese heritage about the way Chinese immigrants did the brutal work of building the US transcontinental railroad while not being fully welcomed or respected.

Last year I visited Bryan Stevenson in Montgomery, Alabama. His work involves exonerating innocent death row victims, and he has created a project to remember African American victims of lynching. His team has been collecting jars of soil from the hundreds of sites where the murders happened. He wants to be sure this story—these stories—are remembered as essential to truth, repentance, reconciliation, and creating a better story together.

When we know our story and the way it interacts with other people's stories, part of it is likely uncomfortable (when ancestors oppressed others), part will guide us to empathy (our ancestors were once downtrodden and oppressed too), and all of it should inspire us to be a part of telling a story that rolls forward into history like a river of liberation and justice.

Last summer with immigrants, refugees, and the ideas of friends like Lisa in mind, during our family vacation in North Carolina we drove by a sign that announced the Scottish Highlands Festival was happening near the cabin where we were staying. I wanted to go ethnic searching. The kids were ambivalent. My North Dakotan/Scandinavian/Welsh wife wanted to hike to a waterfall instead of parking, riding a bus up a mountain, and then paying to walk around booths selling expensive kilts (hundreds of dollars to tap into tartan authenticity) and refusing to eat haggis. They kindly gave in to my wanting to go.

While there, it was fascinating how much our kids, who know a little about their heritage because their grandfather talks about it from time to time, were excited to learn about our last name and what area it's from. Bagpipers paraded around in loud piping bands. Burly shirtless men threw telephone poles. Kilts were everywhere and my kids thought it funny that some of the guys presumably wore nothing underneath. (I might have prepared them for this by showing them the clip of *Braveheart* when those fighting for independence turned around and mooned the British army.)

They were disappointed that the Annans were considered a District Family, not part of a clan. It turns out that a majority of Scots weren't part of a clan. My daughter was comforted when the grandmother sharing about our heritage said District Families were generally more peaceful and better educated. That was not the way to sell my son on our heritage. But he did like that some kilt-wearers were also wearing small daggers.

Why is this useful?

My wife is Scandinavian and Welsh. My family, I'd always understood, is mostly Scottish and English. So one way this can help Americans to be aware of our own story is that, of course, we too are immigrants, and also the measure of things is not being "white." *That could be me* is actually *that was us* when it comes to immigration, which should shape our desire to welcome.

Lisa Sharon Harper also suggests that DNA testing can help keep us from thinking of "white" as a category (and too often the defining category) in the United States. I shipped off my spit to one of the big

DNA testers and received these results: 37 percent Great Britain, 20 percent Ireland, 19 percent Scandinavian, 18 percent Western Europe, and 5 percent stretching into Eastern Europe.

When we know our family's story—going back a generation or two as well as stretching back through history—chances are we have reasons to feel pride and reasons to cringe. And the reason for this self-awareness is that we ultimately want to be part of a Magnificent Story—a story of goodness, beauty, and truth. Loving our neighbors who are suffering isn't the only plot in this magnificent story, but it is a big and essential one because of divine love for people in these circumstances. One way to take part in the Magnificent Story is to live by grace and welcome our immigrant and refugee neighbors—and thereby welcome, and be welcomed, by God.

STORIES THAT CHANGE US

Hearing these stories, stepping closer to their experiences, makes a difference.

"Thank you for listening to my story," Farah said to us in her living room in Mafraq, Jordan, after she shared for a couple of hours in compelling, painful detail about her escape from Syria to be a refugee there. Bombs exploded so loud and so near. She grabbed her children. She ran for her life with her children, including a sprint through four dangerous blocks "that felt like I was running for a year."

As we finished visiting, we thanked her for sharing her story. Then she thanked us.

"When you listen to my story, it gives me some relief to share it," she said. "I also tell my story because of the other people—not just Syrians, but all of humanity, who face this kind of suffering. Maybe when others hear this they will help other refugees."

She relieved a tiny bit of her own burden by sharing her story with us—but also did it because she felt the burden of obligation toward others.

Likewise, when we hear, we receive the holy privilege of being transformed ourselves by her story, doing our tiny part so she doesn't carry her story alone. Then we also share in this responsibility to do something for her and for others, like she said, who are in the midst of similar suffering right now.

These are the kinds of stories that can change our—and other people's—hearts and minds:

Stories from afar. Many people are far away, like those telling the three stories that opened this chapter. But we can let their experiences shape us if we pay attention to the need to do justice and love kindness.

Stories of God. This is the Magnificent Story that we believe we're part of that gives us life and that we want to keep on changing us. Central to God's love story with humanity is a group of people fleeing captivity in Exodus and wandering in search of home. Then when they found home they were supposed to welcome the stranger. Jesus continues the plot, saying that when you welcome the stranger, you welcome him.

The story of reality. Make sure we're getting the true story and addressing real concerns (remember the last chapter), even as people on different sides try to manipulate facts for their own purposes.

Stories of people we're close to. Who we're close to shapes who we are, maybe most of all. If you know people who have had experiences like in those three stories earlier in this chapter, they probably have an even deeper impact on you.

The story of ourselves. Reflecting on our own story can open our minds to new ideas, open our eyes to blind spots in our own view of the world, and open our hearts to new compassion.

Farah invites us to carry her story with her and also to keep living a better story ourselves. Throughout this book we're touching on all the kinds in the list above and how *their stories* can transform *our story.*

TERRIBLE RESPONSIBILITY TRANSFORMED
INTO A MAGNIFICENT STORY

It's unlikely you or I will ever be in a lecture hall and have a revelation like Nicholas Winton received—where everyone whose life you touched stands up from their seats around you in gratitude for the difference you made to them. How fantastic and encouraging that would be!

Yet our lives can be similar to his. History probably won't have thrust us into such extreme circumstances, but if we pay attention and listen closely, we face our own moments of opportunity to confront suffering.

When we follow Jesus, we join a story of death being raised to new life, and, as the prophet Isaiah says, of belonging and hope in which "your light shall break forth like the dawn, and your healing shall spring up quickly. . . . The LORD will guide you continually . . . you shall be called the repairer of the breach, the restorer of streets to live in" (Isaiah 58:8, 11, 12).

As we live into this story, we can welcome someone who has had to step into the unknown—like the man on the boat, so he finds belonging and a safe way out of the middle of the existential and literal sea.

We can welcome someone who is a daughter without ripping away her loved ones—so families aren't separated, and those who are separated are brought back together.

We can welcome someone like Joseph who displays grit and courage in the face of near impossible odds. We can also welcome those who are weighted under depression, PTSD, or the sadness of loss, so they can be cared for and maybe rediscover some of their grit and dreams.

We can choose to listen to Scripture, our own family's story, facts, and to other people's experiences from near and far so that we're shaped by the most important stories: the ones that connect us into the Magnificent Story.

At the end of the interview with *60 Minutes*, the interviewer emphasizes to Mr. Winton that all of these children—and now their children and grandchildren—are only alive because of him.

"Terrible responsibility, isn't it?" he replies, with both gravitas and a twinkle in his eye.

Indeed, it's a terrible but wonderful responsibility that we have to listen and respond to the lives of refugees and immigrants. They might never have the chance to meet you. Yet these are some of the people who one day could stand up and say, "You welcomed me."

PRACTICE

Learn Someone Else's Story

This practice is to spend time with someone who has had a refugee or immigrant experience—so you can hear his or her story.

Is there someone in your life who is an immigrant or refugee who you know a little, but whose story you've never really heard? Someone at church? A work colleague? A neighbor a few houses down? If so, see if one of them would be interested. If not, talk with a friend who knows someone and you can do it together.

The invitation, especially in our nation's climate now, has to be done with care so they don't think you're an immigration official or investigating for some reason. For good reason, there is a lack of trust and we need to respect that. But if possible, invite someone and say, "We've known each other for a long time, and I know you're from _____. But I've never heard your story. It seems like these days in our country it's important to get to know each other better. Could I buy you lunch, or would you like to come over to our home for dinner and share your story about where you come from, what your home is like, how you came? If not, I understand, and no problem. But if so, it would be an honor to hear more of your story."

There can be language barriers, with awkward silences you just sit through, that make it hard to go very deep. There are gender issues, where it's not appropriate to have some of these conversations between men and women. There can be painful parts of the story that people do or don't want to talk about. Many refugees suffer from PTSD. It usually takes more effort for less immediate reward than being with friends. All this is part of the listening.

We treat the person as a person made in God's image every moment, with the deepest respect. We want this practice to be driven by love for them, not by what we'll get out of it. We listen and see where it goes. And we see whether or not it will happen again. You can complement this practice by reading a more in-depth news story than you normally would or find a documentary that tells an immigrant or refugee story. But in this practice we want to listen to someone's story in person—for his or her sake and to see where it might lead us.

GETTING
PRACTICAL

How can we not see the face of the Lord in the face of
the millions of exiles, refugees, and displaced persons
who are fleeing in desperation. . . . For every one of
them, each with a unique face, God reveals himself
always as the one who courageously comes to our aid.

POPE FRANCIS, ON GOOD FRIDAY

The man goes wobbly. Recovers. Then collapses to the pavement.

He tries to get back up.

Collapses again.

The finish line is near but impossibly far. He's trained so hard and given up so much to go these twenty-six miles. Now, with just three hundred yards to go, everything in him has surrendered except his will. His body can't take another step.

As we watch him suffer, our hearts go wobbly too.

Then a fellow runner puts his arm around him and helps him, step by tenuous step, toward the finish line. Not someone from the crowd. Not someone in an Event Staff T-shirt. It is a runner who has trained hard and run far and wants the reward of clocking a good time, but then he slows to help instead of pressing to the finish line. We witness the beauty of trying, the tragedy of collapse, the courage of still pushing to finish, and the generosity of a stranger slowing down to help.

Have you seen a video of this kind of scene near the end of a marathon? The most recent I saw was of the London marathon.

David Wyeth was near the London Marathon's finish line when his legs gave out. He crumpled to the ground. He tried to get up and fell again.

Matthew Rees was running up alongside him and thought, "This is more important—getting him across the line is more important than shaving a few seconds off my time."

Matthew encouraged David, but David kept falling over because he wasn't very coherent. Matthew put his left arm around his waist and pointed toward the finish line. David's exhausted body and mind fumbled as though he were extremely drunk.

They take it step by step together in front of a large white columned building, with a crowd on both sides. Clearly David cannot do this on his own. A race worker in a red Adidas jacket jogs up to help as well.

David's arm then goes up over Matthew's shoulder for better support. David's other arm goes over the race worker's shoulder.

Dozens of runners go past them toward the finish line. The three of them keep making their way the last 150 yards or so.

The crowd is cheering for everyone, but maybe especially for David. Matthew waves his hand up for the crowd to cheer more to encourage David. When you have nothing left, the backing of others can give you strength to keep going.

When they cross the line, another red-jacketed race worker steps in. Matthew deftly steps out from under David's arm and the worker steps under. Three steps later a paramedic receives them. Two other paramedics quickly join them to care for David.

Matthew has veered off, leaving the workers to give David the care he now urgently needs.

In these two and a half minutes, we see the end of a marathon. But we also glimpse a picture of life's marathon of justice. The marathon of a refugee. Of an immigrant. The courage and generosity, the suffering and collapse, the need for someone else to help you across the finish line.

Most people don't stop to help the person who is wobbling and collapsing in these circumstances. They're exhausted themselves and focused on finishing as best they can. Yet the *most inspiring* moment happens when a runner slows to help a fellow runner who can't make it any farther alone.

It's the beauty of one human at the end of her limits being met by another human who is at her best. I like an Olympic backstory as much as the next person. And if the favorite wins, or Michael Phelps swims for his 143rd gold metal, that's great and there's probably a heroic tale of struggle and discipline behind their victory. Someone won this London marathon, and I guess I'm happy for that person. But for the human story, nothing is more beautifully illuminating than the pain and love, the vulnerability and generosity of Matthew helping David across the finish line. That story leads us into the kind of partnering we can do with immigrants and refugees.

In earlier chapters we looked at the importance of recognizing the stranger—as well as addressing our own concerns. Matthew recognized David's need. Then he put his arm around him. Actually, he seemed to have moved along the Good Samaritan Scale, partly through his empathy, realizing *that could be me*. "My calf started to cramp really early on," said Matthew, "so I just decided, 'I've just got to make it to the finish line,' and so when I saw the guy on the floor it sort of brought the feelings I'd had the whole marathon to me."

In this chapter we look at partnering, which we glimpsed as Matthew helped David finish with the most dignity and agency possible. He gauged whether he should just encourage, just help him up, or just put an arm around the waist, and found that he needed to fully support David. Then the professional in the red jacket came and joined in. When they crossed the finish line, other experts stepped in, and Matthew moved out of the way so they could check David's level of dehydration and exhaustion, get all his vital signs. Matthew later checked in on David to be sure that he was okay.

I don't plan to ever run a marathon, but there are good practical ways to partner with refugees and immigrants to help them along their marathon and across the finish line. Yet we know that even as they make it across one finish line (even with heroic effort), in reality they're then immediately starting another marathon in a new home.

Actually, I mentioned earlier that on average a refugee is a refugee for more than ten years. So if you also add in the resettling or starting new in another country, instead of twenty-six miles, their marathon sometimes lasts closer to twenty-six years.

Like Matthew, even as we run our own marathons, we want to be ready to welcome and help others along the way. We ask ourselves: *What race are we really trying to run here?* That is also a question of the apostle Paul who spoke at least twice about finishing the race (1 Corinthians 9:24; 2 Timothy 4:7).

WHAT RACE?

I want to run the race in which, at the end of my life, I hear the words, *You welcomed me into your life so we could run, walk, or limp forward together by God's grace.* Do you? *Together* we have a better chance of running the right race and running it well, to the end.

We'll now look at practical ways we can help locally, nationally, and internationally. Then we'll look at how we can be good partners. All of this is an invitation to be part of a beautiful story of making it step by step toward the finish line together.

LOCALLY

One afternoon as I was writing this book in our local library, I found myself increasingly annoyed by people talking loudly in the cubicle next to me. I was sputtering to myself, couldn't concentrate, about to ask them to quiet down.

Then I recognized they were doing English lessons. A gray-haired white woman of about seventy-five was doing language lessons with a Latina woman about twenty-five. They were talking very loudly, repeating the words. The older woman was volunteering to help the younger woman in a way that would help her integrate locally and help her career.

I laughed at my selfish impulse and hypocrisy—like the ice cream man getting annoyed at kids too happily enjoying their delicious ice cream. So I kept working with a smile as their conversation tumbled through the thin wall. Frustration turned into inspiration.

How we recognize the people we see—the story we see them in—makes all the difference. Here are some ways you can help.

Volunteer with language tutoring or helping kids in school, like the women and men in the small library cubicles next to me and at the church we'll hear about in the next chapter.

Offer pro bono services directly to immigrants or refugees or to organizations that are supporting them. This can be as a carpenter, a lawyer, a human resources expert, a mechanic, and so on.

Hire refugees or immigrants in your business.

Give money to help local groups who are addressing immigrant and refugee needs. This may take some research to find out what services take place locally, which is part of the process of learning about the local support that is or isn't available.

Organize for your church, business club, soccer team, or community organization to learn and serve locally through a local or national organization that can guide you to the best ways to help.

Advocate for local policy that welcomes people well. This can be done individually and with churches or local groups. It helps to have a leader who is very involved or to work with an organization that can provide guidance for how to be most effective.

Make your business welcoming to the local immigrant community. I once visited a huge apple orchard in Washington State. There were apples everywhere: down endless rows of trees (six thousand acres of apple and cherry trees) and scooting across conveyer belts to be packaged. The Broetje family had developed a local school, community center, and many other projects to welcome and support the immigrant community, including both the permanent and migrant, who are colleagues in their business. Their children went to the same school. Their vision of partnering offered insights and inspired.

Welcome a refugee. This is a serious commitment, of course. It involves partnering with a resettlement agency and years of commitment. For example, after the initial burst of energy, Lutheran Immigration and Refugee Service helps communities sustain their hospitality. They call this the "Long Welcome"—the process by which newcomers are received and eventually integrated into their communities. Churches I've visited talk about the joy of receiving, and how it is a long-term commitment that has to keep going past the energy of first welcome. They also talk about the transformative experience for their community, opening their eyes in many ways.

Be a friend. This may be the most demanding because many of us have little spare time. It doesn't have the same quick, tangible payoff as finding a couch to deliver to a family who would otherwise have to sit on the floor. To help someone through loneliness, to sit on their couch, to eat their food—that requires commitment and patience. Have them over to sit and eat. Listen haltingly across languages. Sometimes it's less about doing than about just being a friend.

NATIONALLY

Historically our nation has welcomed and provided opportunity for many but also enslaved or rejected many others. Many things have improved, but with our conflicted history, with a stream of white supremacy still flowing, with the cost of exploitation and discrimination still being paid, and with a divided vision for our country, we still have so far to go.

We talked in chapter three about confession as a way to be formed by and freed into love, which can help move us forward personally and also as a nation. We lament parts of our history but aren't paralyzed; we have the opportunity to work for reconciliation and to keep getting better.

Here are some additional ways to help our country become more welcoming for immigrants and refugees.

We can advocate for national policy that helps improves the lives of refugees and immigrants. Connect with a group like World Relief, International Rescue Committee, or Lutheran Immigration and Refugee Service and ask to be on their advocacy team. You can share with them what you're available to do. For example, you can be alerted to make a phone call every few months (five minutes tops) to call your government officials when an important piece of legislation is up for vote that will affect people's lives. You can call to oppose a policy like separating young children from their parents when they seek asylum at the border, and when enough of us speak up, we saw it can make a difference.

We can ensure a tone of love by speaking well of the refugees and immigrants we know. We can avoid or call out demeaning language. We can model love in our conversation. I heard someone say that once after he preached about refugees, at the end of the service he stood at the church door shaking people's hands as they left. One said he had a gun on him, right at that moment, and that *these people* needed to get out of our country. Then a young Chinese person said they were so grateful for the words of welcome. Another mixed-race couple came out, also grateful. All at the same church. Like our actions, our words matter. We may have different positions on policy and politics, but our words matter and can be deeply encouraging for people who don't feel welcomed.

We can make culture. In *Culture Making,* Andy Crouch helpfully frames change not as a fight against the negative (culture wars) but as an opportunity to create something new (culture making). This is a more effective and joyful way to live and serve God's kingdom. As we get involved locally, nationally, and internationally, we're creating a culture of welcoming. A good example of this is Refuge Coffee in Clarkston, Georgia, which I mentioned in chapter two. I talked there with Leon, a refugee from the Democratic Republic of Congo, and Frey, a refugee from Somalia, who were both serving coffee. This hipster-looking coffee spot creates stories of welcome, which helps people reach across their concerns to join in this story of being friends and allies.

We can vote. We need to consider many issues when we vote, but we shouldn't just vote based on self-interest. We should vote to love our neighbors—especially neighbors such as immigrants and refugees who are most vulnerable.

We can support national organizations that are doing good work on our behalf. When we enable their work through prayer, time, and/or money, then they can use their expertise to make good things happen that we believe in.

INTERNATIONALLY

Most refugees won't make it to the United States, Canada, Australia, or Europe. Which is a good thing. Ultimately it's better and more cost efficient for care to be provided near their homes. And hopefully they will be able to return home when the conflict or famine, or whatever the situation, ceases.

When I worked for four months in northern Albania, I was humbled by a small church of about sixty people who were committed to helping their refugee neighbors who had fled the violence in Kosovo. They were living in challenging circumstances themselves. They packed food, delivered mattresses, and many even gave up rooms in their small homes or apartments to welcome others. Despite living at a far lower standard of living than most Americas, they were giving generously of themselves—and always seeking more ways to give.

When I was in northern Uganda, I was amazed at how Uganda, the United Nations, nonprofits from the United States and around the world, and local Ugandans were helping people from South Sudan.

Think back to our opening story of the marathon runner. Think of how awful you would feel if you were in David's condition, out of steam and stumbling toward the end, unlikely to make it, feeling empty in every way—and then people started jeering at you, calling you names, painting you with a discouraging, defaming brush.

We have to be better as a country, from the highest levels of government to the lowest level of Facebook and Twitter comments.

The ways we can help internationally are limited but important.

Give money to organizations serving refugees internationally. Most refugees are going to a nearby country that doesn't have enough resources to receive them. (At the end of the book I'll give recommendations.)

Connect through these international organizations to ways you can advocate for others, in some ways similar to the local and national approaches above.

Change the conversation when others speak in demeaning ways so that we're always respecting the dignity of displaced people and those wanting to escape suffering to provide a better life for their family. We make a difference when we positively hold up the image of God in others and when we're able to share basic facts and positive stories in the face of denigrating narratives about other people. We can change the conversation toward good.

BEING A GOOD PARTNER

As we take practical action to help, it's important to think about how to do it well. The phrase the "Long Welcome," referring to refugee resettlement, brings to mind Eugene Peterson's book *A Long Obedience in the Same Direction*.

Often when we partner for justice, there is an imbalance of power. Someone is vulnerable and needs help. So we want to help, which is great. But it's always important to see helping not just as a burst of compassion, but also a long obedience in the same direction.

Here are some principles guided by the philosophy that we should partner *with* people and not *for* them, whether in a momentary struggle as with that stumbling marathoner or over the long-term with a family trying to make a new home out of nothing.

We listen humbly so we can understand people and their circumstances that in many ways differ so much from us and our circumstances. Listening should guide our helping.

We're open-eyed about the context, which means we're paying attention to power dynamics, the history of their community and ours, and anything else that might have an effect on their situation and feelings, including our interaction.

We count the partnering cost so we're ready to offer the long welcome that can keep us going past the early compassion adrenaline.

We prepare for angels and demons so we're aware that both we and the people we're helping have a mixed capacity as sinners and saints. Let's be ready and prepared for this, not surprised. This principle relates to not flattening people into caricatures of victims needing our help. They and we are fully human.

We prepare the way for their agency. We're doing our best to prepare a way for them to make their own way into thriving as people in their community. This also includes taking the long view, so we're not forcing things but letting them emerge in a healthy way.

We build trust, knowing that we learn that from each other.

We spread credit around so partnerships are always nourishing and encouraging to everyone involved.

This approach to listening and partnership leads to inspiring, practical help. I have seen people like Danielle in her community in Portland, where she's such a thoughtful friend and advocate for refugees who are neighbors. I've seen the same with Scott and others I met there, and with the Refuge Coffee community in Atlanta. Then there are Matt and Beth in the Chicago suburbs. And in Jordan, Maggie and Jeanette, who had tears streaming down her cheeks as she talked about the injustice caused by the nuances of work permits. Jeanette wants to fix this problem for the refugees she works with, but it's so hard. Isaac and Sarah and others in northern Uganda have shown me the way Ugandans, South Sudanese, and foreigners work together to improve the lives of an overwhelming number of people who had to flee their homes. The woman in the library cubicle next to mine is partnering with an immigrant, in this case to help her English improve. The legal advocates working late hours also protect people's dignity and rights. The list could go on to name dozens, hundreds, and even thousands and thousands of people. When we take practical action, we join in a cloud of witnesses to God's love for us and for others.

"In the United States, the average refugee becomes a net contributor to public coffers eight years after arrival. The assistance they received when they arrived was, in purely monetary terms, an investment with a positive return . . . [and] refugees actually pay back more in taxes than what they receive in benefits—about $21,000 more in the first 20 years in the United States."

Partnering well to welcome our neighbors should be more about accomplishing good—and particularly about facilitating the agency of people so they can shape their own lives—than about feeling good.

Churches who have welcomed refugees told me, "Now we can't imagine our church without them." It's like after getting married, like after a child is born, or like foster parenting. After we welcome the very best into our lives it's so much more complicated and demanding than we could ever have known, but also so much richer that we can't imagine life without welcoming.

About 1 million immigrants come to the United States each year. By region of birth, immigrants come from South and East Asia (27%), Mexico (27%), Europe/Canada (14%), the Caribbean (10%), Central America (8%), South America (7%), the Middle East (4%), and sub-Saharan Africa (4%).

JUSTICE IN ACTION, BEAUTY IN MOTION

When you zoom out and look at our world, the evil and suffering can be overwhelming. But so can the good.

I'm on the board of a charitable foundation. Every four months we read a 250-page packet of proposals from nonprofits working with vulnerable children, mostly in Cambodia, Haiti, and the Appalachian region of Tennessee. Usually I do my reading in one day in the airports and on planes on the way to the meeting. I find it a spiritually invigorating and exhausting process.

On one hand, it feels like being too close to the chill of the Ringwraiths, those shadowy horsemen in the Lord of the Rings—"darkness went with them, and they cried with the voices of death"—when reading about children who are sexually exploited by twisted men (mostly men), labor abuse, lack of educational opportunities, and so on. But then right along with that dark chill is the warm Spirit breathing hope as I read on the same pages about, for example, a Cambodian professor training a new generation of social workers to help their country. I see the spectacular beauty of love in action evidenced by careful thought, problem solving, improvisation, faithful action, collaboration, generosity, and continual improvement.

It's like the despair-hope whiplash of going from Haiti back to the United States in only two hours and noticing the beauty and suffering on both sides in such extremes.

I felt some of this despair-hope whiplash while spending a day in the Chicago suburbs with a national nonprofit, World Relief, but mostly I was struck by the beauty of their doing justice, loving mercy, and walking humbly with God and neighbor.

When we arrived at a church they partner with, I thought about how our country is receiving fewer refugees and how the deportation crackdowns mean Latino/a children aren't showing up for valuable educational and health services all over the country because their parents fear immigration officers' raids. An unholy chill indeed.

But as this agency, which settles about 10 percent of the United States' refugees, shares about their work, it's beautiful. By day's end I thought of them as an outstanding orchestra: hundreds of instruments coming together to play music that lifts our souls toward God. Only more beautiful.

The nine US national refugee resettlement agencies are

- Church World Service
- Episcopal Migration Ministries
- Ethiopian Community Development Council
- HIAS (the global Jewish nonprofit that protects refugees)
- International Rescue Committee
- Lutheran Immigration and Refugee Service
- US Committee for Refugees and Immigrants
- United States Conference of Catholic Bishops, Migration and Refugee Services
- World Relief

As of the time of this book's publication, this list is accurate, though many expect that some of these agencies will be cut by the US government in the months ahead.

I talked with staff members about how they facilitate church and volunteer involvement. In an old Methodist church, children and women and men from around the world are being tutored in English by volunteers. It's a 35 percent Hispanic community that has also been settled by Syrian, Bhutanese, Congolese, Iraqi, and other refugees. A young woman from Afghanistan, wearing a hijab, shared about her struggles and all she had accomplished already during her first year in the United States, including her work in a local factory.

The resettlement process is impressive, from arrival to language learning to job training to job placement. Incredible commitment and competence from our government agencies, nonprofits, and local volunteers make this possible. (Though this whole infrastructure is under duress because of how few refugees are now being welcomed.)

Another refugee resettlement agency (nine agencies have been doing resettlements in the United States) describes their scope of work like this: protection through legal and physical support in the early stages; stabilization so people can independently meet their own basic needs through information and resources; integration with social and economic opportunities; and the long welcome by which people truly come to belong and are able to do well.

Later we drove from the church to the settlement agency's office. I met people in the finance department who ensure good stewardship so donor gifts make a difference for immigrants and refugees. I met with pastors who have seen their churches transformed by helping refugees, and heard how refugees' lives have been changed. At one of our last meetings, I sat with ten people in the legal department who talked about how they help immigrants and refugees, from the citizenship process, to escaping domestic abuse situations, to many cases in between. I thanked the legal team and told them my daughter currently wants to be a lawyer when she grows up. Unexpectedly, I choked up when I told them I'd be proud if my daughter followed in their footsteps.

We're going to be disappointed, people are going to get deported, and other heartbreaking events will happen. But brilliant light shines when we take practical steps toward change and see the story of love in action in our country and around the world.

The light won't prevent the dark chill from coming, but working together, the light—as we're guided by the Light of the World—can overcome the darkness.

RUNNING TOGETHER IS THE RIGHT RACE

For the last two and a half minutes of the London marathon broadcast, commentators were focused on Matthew helping David toward the finish line. Another runner who had completed the race was there in the broadcast booth as they marveled at Matthew's sportsmanship and as the crowd cheered them.

As they watched Matthew and David cross the line, the runner said candidly, "I saw a couple of people in real trouble [when I was running], and I gave them a pat on the bum when I ran past and said, 'Keep going' rather than stop and carry them over. So I'm feeling slightly guilty and selfish having watched people give up their race to help somebody who has emptied their tanks totally."

This was a moving and honest confession at the end of those few minutes watching these two runners cross the finish line. The runner who had passed by others without helping was wondering, in essence, if he was running the wrong race.

Yes, more important than finishing first is finishing together. More important than the fastest time is running the right race. When I talked with Americans, Jordanians, Ugandans, and others involved in welcoming as individuals and as churches and as nations, they didn't hide that it is often a long, hard process and that the work of welcoming extends far past the initial burst of compassion. But they also said it was worth it.

"I have fought the good fight, I have finished the race, I have kept the faith," says the apostle Paul (2 Timothy 4:7), and this isn't a race that we win alone—and it's not a race we win quickly. We win when, by grace, we run the long welcome together.

PRACTICE
Taking a Step

For this practice, here are three questions for you to consider when discerning how you can help:

1. What is an effective way I can partner for change?

2. Which way am I drawn to help right now with the gifts I have, with the time I have for it, and where I find joy in meeting a real need?

3. How can I be a good partner as I do this?

To take your next steps, pick one thing to try in each of the categories—local, national, international. As you choose something from each category, you're listening to the Spirit and to the people whose stories have moved you as you pick what you would enjoy doing (even if it feels like it will stretch you a bit).

Locally I will:

Nationally I will:

Internationally I will:

Then as you do each of these things, consider how you can be a good partner in this—so you're partnering *with* and not *for*, so you're picking people and organizations who partner respectfully with the immigrants and refugees they serve.

We listen, we help, we feel joy, we stumble, we learn along the way, and we see where it leads our partnering next.

FORM A
HUMAN CHAIN

*We must learn to live together as brothers, or
we will all perish together as fools.*

MARTIN LUTHER KING JR.

*F*orm a human chain!"

A powerful rip current had pulled ten people—a family and four other swimmers who tried to help—out to sea. The current at this Panama City, Florida, beach was too strong. They couldn't swim back in. They were crying out for help for a long time, with nobody noticing.

"Form a human chain!" people started shouting as they realized that would be the only way to save them from drowning. By the time people on the beach noticed, the situation was urgent. They couldn't swim out to save them because of the current. The group had been out there about twenty minutes, including eight- and eleven-year-old boys.

At first only five people started the chain, which didn't get even close to where the need was. Then fifteen. Soon dozens of people were stretching out into the ocean. Getting closer. Some couldn't swim themselves but were holding each other by the wrists and arms. Eventually a human chain of more than eighty people made it out to the struggling swimmers.

They passed the swimmers back along the links, through the churning sea that wanted to take them away, take them under. All the swimmers, and all the rescuers, made it back safely to shore.

They walked back out of the water, women and men, different ethnicities. What a beautiful scene of working together to help each other. None of them—those needing saving, those seeking to save—could have done this alone. Every link was necessary.

Jesus told a story about a sheep that gets lost. The shepherd goes out with determination to find it. When he does, "He lays it on his shoulders and rejoices." Jesus then says, "There will be more joy in heaven over one sinner who repents than over ninety-nine righteous persons who need no repentance" (Luke 15:5, 7).

There is great joy in one being found—joy too abounds when one of God's children is saved from the water, or from the conflict zone, or from the famine. Whenever we turn in the right direction with determination to find and to help others, we meet joy.

Everyone who was part of that human chain must have felt more alive right after they too got back to shore. Don't you think? The Spirit of Life often seems to breathe through us after doing something good for others—even if it's less risky than a human chain!

They faced the desperate situation together and didn't lose hope. The need was urgent, but they had to find a wise approach, even if it took slightly longer, because they couldn't just swim out and get stranded too. So they built a chain strong enough to endure the waves.

It's about the person drowning—but also about each of us committing to do our part until that person is safe.

In this chapter we'll look at how four commitments can renew our strength while we serve as vital links in this human chain:

being good neighbors, siding with hope, seeking reconciliation, and living by grace. Then we can do our part to keep supporting each other, despite the heavy currents, and reach those who need to hear our welcome.

COMMIT TO BEING A GOOD NEIGHBOR—
DESPITE THE RISKS

Mike McClenahan's church is a white middle- and upper-class church in the San Diego area with a thirty-year history of ministering with the area's Hispanic community through tutoring, English classes, and a Hispanic worship service. When the political issue of immigration became hot in 2012, members of the congregation and another pastor formed a group of Spanish and English speakers who shared their stories and read *Welcoming the Stranger*. This led to them wanting the church to consider immigration as a biblical and moral issue that had an impact on many local families, especially the children they were tutoring.

Mike was reluctant. He thought the topic was too political and divisive. Then he heard other pastors and leaders raising the issue, so he invited one of them to preach on Psalm 146 and about how God hears the voice of the vulnerable. Before the sermon, a young man named Juan shared his story of receiving his DACA paperwork so he could complete his master's in marriage and family therapy.

As Juan spoke, Mike stood nervously in the back of the church. When Juan finished, the congregation burst into applause. Mike realized the congregation may be divided on political solutions to immigration, but their hearts were with Juan.

Mike has preached, taught, and given updates occasionally on immigration and refugee issues. When he's received pushback from people who think he is getting too political, talking face-to-face usually helps. Some members have left because of these issues, but others have joined.

It's been worth it. The church tutors over two hundred children from kindergarten to twelfth grade each week. They now offer an immigration service on their campus to help people navigate the challenging legal process. They strive to be a safe, welcoming place for their neighbors, which is important when, for example, children in the tutoring program are showing physical signs of stress due to fear their parents or relatives might be deported. Relationships between the church members and community keep growing, and now immigrants aren't *out there*—they're *in here*. A local or national policy change is no longer just going to impact a stranger. That change will make a huge difference to the child at the water fountain because her dad will be deported. It means a third-grader comes to tutoring but doesn't go to school because papers might be checked.

Mike likes to say, "Because the church is a family in covenant relationship, those children are not just *their* children, they are *our* children. And if they are our children, what will we do differently?"

Our national immigration situation isn't vastly different from other moments in history: 43 million foreign-born people live in the United States, about 13% of the population. Over a hundred years ago, in 1890, the foreign-born population was almost 15% born outside the United States, which is the record immigration level.

Causes for celebration encourage everyone along the way. For instance, the daughter of a longtime facilities staff member at the church went through their program and received a Gates Millennium Scholarship, which will cover her education from an undergraduate degree all the way through a PhD if she wants.

"Our church's story has been shaped by immigrant stories for decades because we've said 'yes' to our neighbors," says Mike. "I don't want to be partisan, but I also can't avoid being political because there are political implications if we follow the gospel and love our neighbors."

"We've also noticed," he says, "that working with immigrants has changed our hearts toward people. When the recent refugee crisis came up we were ready to engage as a church because we were already *welcoming the stranger.*"

As they committed to being good neighbors in their community, those relationships led them to—and continue to renew them in—serving well. They serve as good (Samaritan) neighbors to people around the world.

Research of the past four decades shows that, as immigration increased in American metropolitan areas, on average crimes of murder, robbery, burglary, and larceny decreased. Immigration doesn't increase crime and may actually help reduce it. The most common explanation why is because it revitalizes urban neighborhoods, creating vibrant communities and generating economic growth.

COMMIT TO HOPE—DESPITE THE DESPAIR

In contrast to being set adrift out into a sea of despair, a human chain held together by love and determination helps us to pull each other toward hope.

"Because other people come to be with us," as Archbishop Alapayo had told me as we talked in Uganda. "Only because we're not alone can we find hope."

In South Sudan, he lives in one of the most hopeless places on the planet right now. Yet he still has a spark of joy in him. I don't know how. That human chain, when it reaches into South Sudan or northern Uganda where so many refugees have fled, keeps them linked to hope instead of alone drifting out to sea by losing home, family, job, country.

Almost all of us struggle sometimes to glimpse hope through our darkened window into the world. You don't have to be in the midst of a humanitarian crisis. Middle or upper class, the loss of a child, depression, cancer, and a million other things sap our hope. Life is harder for some, but is in ways a struggle for all of us. When we become part of a chain of welcoming, we can glimpse hope through the shadow. We can see that in some way, even if it looks far away, we're heading toward the shore.

We move toward shore when our lives are being reoriented like that San Diego church was.

We move toward shore where not everything is perfect but where people have security and opportunity and we're wisely addressing bigger, systemic issues.

We move toward shore in a spiritual sense toward Home, always moving with hope. But we also very concretely move toward homes where people can live, be protected, and thrive. This human chain is *a chain of welcoming.*

"If you want to go fast, go alone. But if you want to go far, go together," was the theme at the conference in Uganda where I met the archbishop and about thirty leaders from ten countries in eastern and southern Africa.

We're all in this together to live, love, and learn in service of God's kingdom, which transcends our ethnic group or neighborhood or national borders.

We can make it to the shore together. It takes time and risk, each person doing his or her part. Progress can seem slower than going alone or going just as Americans or going just as white Americans, but the progress that might look fast is no progress at all. That is drifting out into a sea of selfishness and resentment.

We hold tight in our role as part of the human chain; we look to where vulnerable people are who need a hand; and we keep anchored to shore—that is, to our hope. Being committed to hope means being renewed by how fully we're welcomed into God's love, and then letting that determine how we welcome and give others a chance on shore.

COMMIT TO RECONCILIATION—
DESPITE THE FRACTURES

As we commit to being good neighbors and to hope, reconciliation will be needed along the way.

Heather Hayer, at thirty-two years old, gave her life when she was hit by the car of a white supremacist in Charlottesville, Virginia. She was out in the streets to take a stand against this toxic ideology, to show love for her neighbors. That day a group of white men tried to make it clear that "others" were not welcome.

Heather believed differently.

"My daughter . . . had passionate opinions about the equality of everyone," said her dad in an interview shortly after her death.

"People need to stop hating. And they need to forgive each other. I include myself in that, in forgiving the guy who [killed my daughter]. He didn't know no better. . . . I just think of what the Lord said on the cross, 'Lord forgive 'em, they don't know what they're doing.'

"My daughter's life," he continued, his voice starting to break, "I'm proud of her for standing up. She had more courage than I did."

Welcoming isn't always cheap. It costs Ugandans who don't have much extra to share but receive people anyway. It costs Jordanians water when theirs is one of the driest, most water-poor countries in the world. It costs losing something through cultural change, even if we can then create something new and beautiful. Welcoming might cost, but it is the generous way of Jesus.

Forgive us, for we don't know what we're doing—not if we make people who are already suffering as immigrants and refugees suffer more.

We need reconciliation in many profound ways. And one reason is so we can be freed to be better neighbors and serve those who are lost without a home. We approach this humbly because we too are lost in our ways. Welcoming is an activity of lost and found. This is one of the activities of God's kingdom: with the lost sheep, the lost coin, the lost prodigal son who returns from another land to be welcomed home in loving embrace.

Soon before saying, "Forgive 'em, they don't know what they're doing," Jesus told the man next to him, a thief, a loser by any measure, "Today you will be with me in paradise." This is the ultimate reconciling welcome that should inspire us to welcome others.

COMMIT TO GRACE—
DESPITE THE COMPLEXITY

Committing to reconciliation also leads us to committing to grace— that is, to giving, receiving, and being guided by grace.

For a while during this past year I was wrestling through some vocational changes. Melancholy pressed down when I was trying to get up from bed, get up to do good work. It was at the same time as I was writing this book, so then I'd feel guilty about my own malaise as I focused on refugees and immigrants who lost so much, not just who were in a mini mid-life crisis.

Late on more nights than I care to count, after my wife and kids had gone to sleep, I would self-medicate by watching a Netflix series or silly YouTube videos. It's better than excessive drinking or a lot of other options, but still not ideal.

One night, around the same time as the human chain reached out into the ocean across the state from me, I clicked on a clip of *America's Got Talent*. I knew the premise but hadn't seen the show before. Unknown people audition. The bad get made fun of by the sharp-tongued-"just-being-honest"-can-be-an-excuse-for-just-being-mean judge Simon Cowell. The good acts get selected to keep competing together with an opportunity to open doors for their talent.

I clicked.

A young woman stands on stage who looks unlikely to be successful. She's nervous, lacking self-confidence, doesn't look like a pop star. All of us are cringing, judging.

She starts to sing. And it's good. Surprisingly good. Actually it's beautiful. The audience stands. She finishes. The four judges stand applauding too.

Then she starts to cry. And smile. Releasing nerves. And crying more. Joy.

The judges can then vote the contestant off or vote her through to the next stage. But each judge can also hit a golden buzzer, which sends the contestant immediately through.

The buzzer is hit. Golden confetti rains down. She's welcomed. She belongs.

I kept clicking on these.

They're more emotional when it's someone who isn't naturally welcomed by everyone. It's great if the beautiful woman is welcomed, but people tend to welcome supermodels like Heidi Klum, one of the judges, because she's beautiful whether she can sing or not.

When the shy, bungling mechanic gets up to sing, we think he's going to embarrass himself, but then he sings like an angel. In a way he's earned it through talent, but it feels like welcoming grace because usually these people have toiled along for years being unrecognized. Then suddenly, by grace of the show, they're welcomed into open doors.

When the boys who rap about being bullied are welcomed, they're affirmed for turning the very act of being bullied into something lovely and snappy that helps themselves and others stand up against bullying.

The sixteen-year-old with short hair because she's recovering from cancer, for which her own body wasn't welcoming, then sings and moves us. The judges step in on behalf of all of us and say that things are tough, but you are welcomed here.

The woman who lost her hearing at eighteen speaks through a signing translator. She made it through discouragement and at twenty-eight sings an angelic song about continuing to try.

For each of them, the golden buzzer is hit.

The contestant usually shrieks with emotion or bends over with face in hands. Tears stream down. Golden confetti rains in slow motion. One of the songs starts up in the background:

We'll rise up,

In spite of the ache.

We'll rise up,

And we'll do it a thousand times again.

I was moved to tears a number of times. The welcoming. The welcoming.

And I thought of refugees and immigrants who too often receive disdain or indifference. If anyone in the world deserves a Golden Buzzer, they do, right? They've survived. *America's Got Talent* is not a perfect metaphor, but we should rejoice in who refugees are and in all they have accomplished as fellow human beings forced to navigate the worst of circumstances. We should recognize who they are, the journey they've made, the odds against them, all they have lost and overcome, and receive them.

We can genuinely welcome refugees and immigrants into our country. We can help children who were born here to thrive, not to live in fear that their parents will be taken away. We can welcome a Syrian refugee who has lost everything, has gone through vetting, and shouldn't have to then face politicians insulting her in the media or people insulting her on the street.

"We'll rise up," says the song. Tears can well up, yes they can. There is a burst of compassion. But then comes the spiritual work and the partnering work to really welcome.

In my mind, not having seen much of him, I think of the mean version of Simon Cowell as representing those whose ancestors were immigrants (to a land that already had native people) who are now saying a derisive "No!" to other groups who would benefit from coming. But in these golden buzzer scenes, he's authentic and generous and sweet. Let's instead be the best version of Simon and find purpose and joy by celebrating the best of someone else's humanity, seeing them for who they are, and recognizing them not just as a victim or as a threat but as a child of God.

It's not as easy or dramatic as on the TV show, but each of us in our own way can hit the golden buzzer for people. This buzzer affirms with Jesus that the first will be last, and the last will be first. Refugees and immigrants on their own have already had to rise up *a thousand times again.* We welcome when we can as a way to help them rise up yet again.

I mentioned Farah in chapter four. She had thanked us for listening to her harrowing story, as we sipped small cups of very sweet hot tea—or, more accurately, cups of dissolved sugar delivered via tea. We sat on the floor of her living room on thin mats that matched the burgundy curtains hanging over the windows. Outside, the muezzin sang the Muslim call to prayer from speakers in a nearby mosque's minaret.

Farah's home is in Mafraq, a city in Jordan near the Syrian border, which grew from 60,000 to 160,000 people because of the influx of Syrian refugees since the civil war. She was one of them.

Farah was a gracious host, laughing and inviting us in. She wore a head covering, and all her fingers were stained to the first knuckle by henna.

"I'm not nervous to share my story," she said, "but it does make me sad to remember all that has happened."

Her story includes exploding bombs, torture, separation from family and reunion, sprinting for four dangerous blocks holding her child, checkpoint after checkpoint when they thought they might be shot or turned back toward death. It's scary to hear her story, to be entrusted to help her by listening.

Tears streamed down her cheeks at different times in the story. Then she remembered getting to the border.

When she was finally there, Farah sat on the ground and cried. A Jordanian solider came by and picked her up. He wiped her tears.

"Why are you crying?" he said. "You're here now. You're our guest." The soldier took her to get water.

"How else can I help you?" he asked.

"I would love to call my parents," said Farah. "They think I'm dead."

He gave her his phone. She called them. Then she couldn't find the soldier when she finished her call. He had gone off to his other duties.

For hours she searched and finally found him.

"Here is your phone," she said.

"No—why do I want my phone back? You're our guest. It's yours now."

She said wistfully, these several years later, "I've always remembered his face. I would hug and kiss and thank him for what he did for me. I asked if I could go to the border to find him to thank him, but I'm not allowed."

The soldier received her like she deserved the golden buzzer, which she did, though of course there were years of struggle still ahead. Now Farah leads a woman's program to support other Syrian refugee moms so they can be better parents. She was welcomed, though of course she still longs for home. She couldn't find the soldier, but she is helping other refugee mothers to feel more welcomed so that they can make their children feel more welcomed.

Cycles of violence and need disrupt the lives of millions all over the globe and force them to leave home. But cycles of grace, love, and welcoming—like we see in that Jordanian soldier and Farah, as well as so many others—are alive around the globe too, giving comfort to the weary, hope to the hopeless, light to those who feel shrouded in darkness, and belonging to those who are far from home.

YOU'RE VERY WELCOME AND VERY WELCOMED

"You're very welcome," a woman in a white shirt says to me with a big smile and a lovely accent as I walk into the restaurant outside Kampala, Uganda. She seems to work there because a man beside her in a similar white shirt is nodding in agreement.

I look back over my shoulder to see if they're talking with someone else who just thanked them. Nobody is there.

"Um, thank you?" I say.

Then, thoroughly confused, I wonder whether our conversation occurred as it sounds or whether I'd just had a jet-lag-induced memory lapse. *Thank you* and *You're welcome* have been exchanged, but in reverse order. And those were the first words we said to each other. Wait, did I just eat my meal and give a good tip and ... wait, no, they're saying *You're welcome*, so did I express gratitude for a great meal that I haven't eaten yet and then ...?

This confusion flashes through my brain in this restaurant and then in a couple of other exchanges before I figure out that instead of finishing conversations, in this region, "You're very welcome" starts conversations before saying "hi" or any other greeting.

After a few days I'm still not always smooth with what sentence I'm supposed to say to then transition us into conversation, but I love the greeting. There's something deeply hospitable about it. It seems to be saying, "Hi, how are you? We're glad you're here. I'm welcoming you to this place, this moment, to really be with each other."

"You're very welcome" is a great greeting.

"You're very welcome" is a greeting of each person along that chain reaching out into the sea, out into the world, to help those we can.

You're very welcome in my life because I want to listen to you.

You're very welcome in my life because this conversation may become something deeper.

You're very welcome in my life because you're a child of God who is very welcome in God's love and life.

We're welcomed by God's love—and so by grace we practice welcoming; we fail; we break through; we keep practicing.

We grow in faith and love by welcoming others. It would be great if our efforts were completely selfless, but know that's not realistic. But we can commit to helping in order to help, and also helping because it helps to shape us in the way of Jesus. This is the long obedience toward Love. This is hope in the way Love can work through us to help others, and through others to help us. We meet God together.

One American I talked to who has spent most of his career in other countries helping refugees told me he experiences grace alongside the sadness and hard work: "Hearing what they've experienced is like walking close to death without it stealing you away. They remind you what is most important."

At the end of a trip to Jordan, during a particularly stressful personal time, I had a few hours in the hotel before a midnight flight. Suddenly my heart started to race. I felt anxious. I felt like I might pass out. I opened my room door and sat on the floor so that if I passed out another guest would find me.

But passing out or something more serious felt more possible by the minute. Was this stress, exhaustion from traveling, dehydration, some mix? A heart problem? Something worse? After five or ten minutes nobody walked down the hallway, and I figured the hotel wasn't busy enough for anyone to find me lying halfway out my room on the floor. So I shuffled down to the lobby and sat where staff walked by regularly. I knew I was in bad form in shorts and a T-shirt as women walked by in black hijabs with only their eyes visible, but I didn't want to risk going back into my room and falling over. If I fell over down in the lobby, they'd see me and help or take me to the hospital.

And what was going through my mind during this panic attack or whatever it was?

I was talking to God, and all I wanted was to be at home with my wife, daughter, and son. I needed to be there. I wanted to be with them. I wanted to be holding them and being held. I wanted to be home. I thought of the people I'd been talking with in Uganda and in Jordan. I wanted them to be home, to be with each other, knowing that many had lost loved ones, parents, and children.

In a couple of hours I felt better (though I never did learn what caused the episode) and could board the plane toward home.

The grace we can receive in experiences that make us reflect about our mortality and what is most important, as well as in conversations with those who have lost everything, is the stripping away of false promises of perfect security, purity, or prosperity that will come if we just take care of our own. We can then see more clearly the way toward God's kingdom coming—a way of love and welcoming.

Jesus doesn't explain God's kingdom. He hints, tells stories. It's like the widow finding a coin. The shepherd finding a sheep. Like a seed being planted. And maybe it's like more than that too.

Maybe this kingdom is like a human chain reaching out into the ocean to help one back to shore who is almost lost. Loving our immigrant and refugee neighbors means finding our place in the chain of people that can rescue them from an undertow that isn't letting them swim to shore.

Maybe the kingdom is like holding a stranger's hand as an airplane takes off, or lifting a classmate out of her bed to help her into her wheelchair, or like saving orphans from a concentration camp, or putting an arm around a fellow racer to help him to the finish line.

Maybe the kingdom is like pressing a golden buzzer so a child of God knows she belongs and is welcome to flourish and share her gifts with her new community.

In all these cases, we need each other. We gain perspective on how small we are, how valuable we are, how we all need to be connected. This isn't wishy-washy, touchy-feely stuff. It's working long, pro bono hours as an immigration lawyer. It's tutoring a thirty-year-old in English. It's working daily in a refugee camp or standing up for unpopular political positions that benefit others but not yourself. It's giving to help someone else welcome a refugee far away.

This is the rigorous commitment of love. This is holding hard to each other and forming a chain even as the current of selfishness and fear and tribalism tries to rip us apart and pull us out into the deep dark sea of selfishness and resentment. Instead we're able to keep holding on despite the strong currents as part of this chain of love and life, because perfect love casts out fear and makes us stronger, able to hold on, able to help those who are adrift and welcome them back to shore.

PRACTICE

Finding Your Place in the Human Chain

1. Reflecting on what you've learned from other practices introduced in previous chapters, what role could you see yourself doing over the next few years as one link in the human chain to serve immigrants and/or refugees? Your time, situation in life, skills, financial resources, and many other factors will be involved—including what breaks your heart, where you glimpse hope, and where God's spirit might be pulling you.

2. A vital part of being a link in the human chain is committing to being a good neighbor, to hope, to reconciliation, and to grace. All of these help us to be very *welcome* and very *welcoming*. What is one small thing in each of these four areas where you can be nourished by God and strengthened to continue in this work:

   a. How can you move along the Good Samaritan Scale by being a *good neighbor* to an immigrant or refugee? This can also extend beyond your own neighborhood.

   b. How can you *nourish hope*, especially when the world's suffering sometimes pushes us toward despair? Related to that is the opportunity to reflect on what motivates you to rest so you can be nourished to really give yourself when you're involved.

   c. How can you take part in conversations of *reconciliation*? Do this with the idea that it's helpful to be self-aware about our stories so we can better help other people's stories move along.

d. Think about how you've received *grace* in your life. Then ask how you can help someone else to experience grace in a similar way.

HERE
IS LIFE

*The highest and most beautiful things in life
are not to be heard about, nor read about, nor
seen but, if one will, are to be lived.*

Søren Kierkegaard

I love it," I said after asking them to repeat it to be sure
I heard correctly. "That's my favorite organization
name ever."

Here Is Life they were called.

We were talking in a sparse classroom as a beige goat
balanced on a ledge just outside the window. We had spent
the day driving several hours in a white SUV on reddish
dirt roads in northern Uganda, near the South Sudan
border at times, to the Bidibidi refugee settlement. I tucked
my feet under my chair so the Here Is Life team didn't see
my (Joseph's) flip-flops. I still felt a mix of awkward embar-
rassment and holy gratitude that I often find is part of
welcoming and being welcomed across various borders.

Here Is Life, they explained, was the name of the organization Isaac (who we met in chapter three) and a few Aringa Christians formed when their tribe returned home after fleeing as refugees themselves in the 1980s.

From the beginning, Here is Life wanted to share the love of Jesus with everyone they could. Now they help refugees who have fled South Sudan. They had built the latrines we'd seen that day. They help with local development and peace-building. It's a name, they say, that declares hope in Christ and shares that hope with others. It declares hope in their community. It commits to the hard work of rebuilding life for themselves and for others, day by day, wherever they are. They are committed to a core value of "sacrificial living in order to enable others to live meaningful lives."

They show that in their country—as in ours—when we address the concerns seriously (as discussed in chapter three), listen to others' stories, reflect on our own stories and on who we want to be, and then commit to helping, we're finding life. Our tribe expands across borders. We're immunized from the "shark attack" mentality that can lead us to dehumanize others. Prudence serves to reduce risk on our way to being as generous as possible. Friendships make us hear changing accents and languages and see changing storefronts differently. They look like overcoming, like achievement, like heroic grit to make an ordinary life.

At another Ugandan refugee settlement, a half-dozen South Sudanese women and men had wanted to show me the church they'd built with mud and sticks. Pews were a single rough-hewn plank held up between two pieces of wood sunk into the dirt floor. The roof was a white tarp with a blue UNHCR logo. They said they pooled their resources—though they barely had enough to survive—to build it. Because even as people without a home, they declared life is *here* by gathering as sisters and brothers to pray and worship.

Their lives open our eyes to where true life is.

Here is life.

LIFE AS NEIGHBORS

Nour Sahawneh is pastor of a church in Jordan near the Syrian border. He is wearing slacks and a short sleeve dress shirt. His phone keeps buzzing from incoming calls and texts. In the crisis he and his church stepped up to receive Syrians coming across the border, people like Farah whose story I shared earlier. The church helped provide basic needs as best they could. That turned into serving as a community center and starting a primary school for Syrian children.

As we stood talking in his church, he told me about the joys and challenges. It's hard to keep up high intensity hospitality over the long-term, he said. Then he says Fort City Church in Fort McMurray, Canada, inspired him along the way.

Fort City Church was deciding to sponsor a Syrian refugee family. They connected with Pastor Nour, who connected them with a family. Within the church were supporters of the idea and skeptics who resisted, mirroring the political divide toward refugees and immigrants in many countries.

Before they could reach consensus and welcome the family, a wildfire raged through Fort McMurray. Almost 90,000 people, basically the whole city, had to evacuate—some driving through flames raging twenty feet high on either side of the road, like a *Fast and Furious* scene turned real and apocalyptic. More than 2,400 homes and buildings were destroyed. Devastating loss.

Who has time to welcome an international refugee family when your community is in crisis? Who can receive others when you're barely on the other side of your own smoke clearing? Dropping the idea would have been completely understandable.

But something unexpected happened. Not only did the church decide to welcome a refugee family, but resistance to welcoming them dropped.

"It was amazing how many people started thinking [about the Syrian refugee family] when they left their own homes that were lost or in danger," said the church's pastor, Doug Doyle. "The reservations [about whether we should welcome them] disappeared when they felt what it was like to be driven out of your home."

The flames refined their somewhat reluctant stance: *Now that we better understand what it is to lose and long for our homes, we want to provide them with a home.* They moved along the Good Samaritan Scale. They responded by deciding, *Here can be new life among the ashes for us—and for others.*

Before arriving in Fort McMurray, Alberta, the Syrian family had been refugees for six years. During the welcome party the first night the woman, who everyone knew was pregnant, pulled one of the Canadians aside and told her it was time. They went to the hospital and she birthed the baby.

"A beautiful example of welcoming," Pastor Nour told me about this church thousands of miles away from him. Yet that church was linked with him and his church by the new life of a family whose child was born just after a plane ride to Canada, and linked by the life of a child who was born two thousand years ago in Bethlehem, about seventy-five miles away from the family's refugee camp.

Sympathy (having pity on people's misfortune, while keeping them at a distance from us) pushes us apart, whereas empathy (seeing the world as other people see it, understanding their feelings, and being vulnerable to their experience) brings us together. The fire had collapsed the distance between this Syrian family and Fort City Church.

We're children of God and our tribe extends beyond "taking care of our own" because Jesus redefined *neighbor* to include anyone who needs us along the proverbial Jericho Road. Before we're Americans or Canadians or Syrians, before we're Republicans or Democrats or Independents, we are neighbors.

Here is life.

LIFE IN BELONGING

My daughter, Simone, doesn't often let me read her bedtime stories anymore. She speed-reads through Rick Riordan's *Percy Jackson* series and other six-hundred-pagers. But I'd met an author who gave me a book she'd written for tweens like my daughter (who *does not* like me using the word *tween*), and eleven-year-old Simone let me read it to her before bed one night: "Jack's father's death . . . memories of his father . . . his father was gone, and so were the adventures they had shared together."

We never read past that first paragraph. That's not the author's fault. Many children's books quickly kill or ship off the parents so the kids are thrust into adventure.

"Dad, you aren't going to leave me, are you? At least not before I'm seventy-five?" she asked at the end of that first paragraph with seriousness wrapped in a joke that soon dissolved into tears—the sweetest, most heartbreaking kind.

"No, I promise I won't leave. Or when I leave, I'll always come back," I said, though we both knew I couldn't fully make the promise, which by then had me verging on tears.

"Okay, so you'll come back from your next trip. But what if tonight a robber comes in? Or if a bomb falls on just your side of the house? Or what if on your trip you get hit by a car when you're crossing the road. Please, please, please promise you won't get hit by a car!"

Her imagination runs to extremes in moments like these, and naming the absurdity aloud helps defang the fear. We were soon laughing through tears. We belong to each other.

Here is life.

"I promise. We'll be safe tonight. But some people aren't. They have to huddle up where bombs drop. They love each other. It must be so hard when they really have to go to bed with these questions, huh? When the worst things really could happen."

I hoped I wasn't doing the emotional equivalent of "there are starving children in Ethiopia" that parents would say to guilt their seven-year-old into finishing their peas.

We prayed for Simone's fears to be soothed, for protection, for dads and daughters, mothers and sons, where a bomb could hurtle down in the middle of the night to rip their lives apart. We prayed for people who have run from places like this. We prayed for God's love and protection to wrap around all of us, all of us, all of us.

Not long afterwards, I read a *New York Times* article titled "Fleeing Boko Haram, Thousands Cling to a Road to Nowhere." Some days I confess I ignore this kind of heaviness, but the title got me: *a road to nowhere.*

It's a desert highway that was built outside Diffa, Niger, then abandoned. It really does not lead anywhere. But 130,000 people have moved to live along this road to flee Boko Haram, the violent Islamist militant group. Yet even this road to nowhere can be turned into a road of belonging for someone else.

Two boys in the article, both my daughter's age, caught my attention. Bana stands in a photo wearing a baggy gray-and-white shirt with his hand on his face. He buys rope then sells it in the market after cutting it into smaller pieces. The other boy is Ibrahim, who returned from a fishing trip with his brother to find their village burned down by Boko Haram. They went village to village for safety. One day his older brother went fishing and didn't come back. Ibrahim was alone at eleven years old, sleeping under a tree.

Abari Koyomi already had fourteen children and grandchildren of his own who he could barely provide for. But he saw Ibrahim, a stranger under a tree, and took him in to live with his family.

"He gave me food. He gave me everything," said Ibrahim. In the midst of being a refugee himself, Abari welcomed Ibrahim to belong in his family.

Here is life.

I talk with my mom every week or two. Sometimes I get updates on the nine-year-old refugee girl with big brown eyes and long brown hair who she's taken to and from about twenty doctor appointments over the past year. She also sits in on the medical appointments to support the girl and her family. A serious fall when she was two left the girl without hearing. She received cochlear implants eight weeks ago and my mom now takes the girl and her family to follow-up visits with a speech pathologist.

Though it's been a serious commitment (Mom doesn't like to drive), my mom only talks about how she's grateful to be part of this family's life and how the little girl and family are finding their way. I'm sure my mom makes them feel like they belong, because in church (my dad's a pastor) and with friends she's famous as a hugger who makes everyone feel like they belong.

The girl's comprehension has kept improving, but she's on a journey of gradual healing because she has been deaf most of her life. She had learned to lip read, so one exercise the speech pathologist has done recently is hold a piece of plastic in front of her mouth as she talks to the girl, because she needs to learn to understand by listening that isn't helped by reading lips.

Here is life, whispers a still small voice into these young ears that are learning to hear.

Juan came to this country as a child. He had no choice. He had no documents. He made it through high school and college. His legal status has vacillated between secure and unsecure, which could lead to deportation. He is now a campus pastor who supports the development and faith of students in this country, the country he knows as home. He has turned his opportunity into a chance to serve others.

Here is life.

Recently in Fairfax County, Virginia, a family went to visit relatives in New York and came back to find their home had been robbed and "F--- Muslims" had been written across the wall.

"We've never felt like we're outsiders or we shouldn't be here," said the Ahmads. But afterward, they told the journalist, "Initially we felt very lonely—this is not the right place for us. We should just move back to Dubai."

A native born-and-raised Fairfax County resident organized a grassroots response that quickly raised $10,000 to help the Ahmads. Neighbors also offered to babysit their children, clean their house, and bring them food.

"We were shocked," said the Ahmads. "Complete strangers, they're doing that for us. We don't feel alone anymore. . . . So many strangers . . . coming forward and donating and offering to help. We feel so loved."

"It's nice to see good outweigh evil sometimes," said the local Fairfax neighbor who organized the response. She wasn't overstating what is at stake.

Here is life.

Friends who are pastors—especially but not only in more post-Christian places like Seattle and San Francisco—have told me many people are prone to "belonging before believing." In other words, they become part of the church community, sometimes for a long time, before they believe the confessions of the church. Making people feel welcomed plays a vital part in the church's call to share the Magnificent Story. "Let your light shine before others, so that they may see your good works and give glory to your Father in heaven," Jesus said (Matthew 5:16). We've seen this light shine throughout the book in the lives of churches and communities, individuals and families. A profound way to testify to God's love is by welcoming immigrants and refugees to belong.

Here is life.

My friend Gustave came to the United States after the 2010 Haiti earthquake because his son Mike was diagnosed with leukemia during the aftermath. They've been here for eight years under Temporary

Protected Status, which the government announced recently will be revoked. He called me proudly a few years ago when he won employee of the month and the hotel where he works gave him a free trip in appreciation. He pays taxes. He attends church. He sends money back to Haiti to help their family. He texted me a couple of months ago to tell me about winning another employee award. He's a good neighbor. After eight years, his four children don't know Haiti. His two older daughters have graduated from high school and are attending college. Many people worked hard to welcome them and to save Mike's life (he's now thirteen and thriving).

Now Gustave is in limbo, scared about going back to Haiti, where it is hard to earn enough to provide well for a family and there is more insecurity for his kids. They made the most of building good lives here because they were welcomed. There is no good reason for their sake or for America's sake—no reason, from economics to compassion—they should have to leave.

"'You are to allot it as an inheritance for yourselves and for the foreigners residing among you and who have children,'" Ezekiel 47:22-23 (NIV) says so beautifully. "'You are to consider them as native-born Israelites; along with you they are to be allotted an inheritance among the tribes of Israel. In whatever tribe a foreigner resides, there you are to give them their inheritance,' declares the Sovereign LORD."

Here is life.

Gustave is one of many friends, colleagues, and strangers from different countries who have kindly *welcomed me* into a deeper understanding of community and hospitality, of God's goodness and grace. It started with people like the refugees from Sierra Leone and Sarajevo with whom I slid around outside in their first snowfall. To be clear, I've often been the one who needs to better understand wealth, privilege, ethnicity, generosity, justice, faith in God. I've found life because they've welcomed me around their table—the communion table and the conversation table—and helped me to belong.

They've helped me to find that in welcoming and being welcomed, *here is life*.

LIFE IN GOD'S LOVE AND PROMISE

One afternoon in Jordan I took a taxi forty-five minutes from Amman to Mount Nebo, where it's thought that Moses stood and looked out over the Promised Land. It is a place of unrequited longing for his new home. He looked but never made it. After forty years of searching and longing, he gazed at what would finally become home. His people would make it, but he wouldn't set foot on the land.

The Bible is a story of liberation, yes, but also of wandering, of homelessness, of seeking, of being immigrants and refugees in strange lands searching for home.

Where I stood, the Dead Sea was off to the left. To the right across the plains were shades of brown and patches of green. Bethlehem lay in the distance. It was deeply moving to stand where Moses stood and see where Jesus was born, to look at land that Jesus' family had fled across as refugees for safety. It was quiet. A bird soared below, between the mount and the Promised Land.

I was mesmerized on Mount Nebo. Only a few other visitors came and went. A monastery and church stand on the mountaintop. They've erected a monument to Moses and Jesus on this spot: Jesus' cross is wrapped by the serpent that Moses put up to heal his people in the desert. The work of finding home doesn't shy from sacrifice or suffering or the profound need for healing.

"There is Palestine, where my family is from," said my taxi driver, pointing across the Promised Land, after I got back in the car. "They came to Jordan in 1947. But our home is over there. My father still has a key. But a Jewish family lives there now."

The longing for home is complex and too often includes conflict along with winners and losers. We wind down through the parched landscape toward the Dead Sea.

A lot of the ugly hate, the violence even, is a perversion of our longing for home—not just in this region of the world, but all over. It surfaces when we think that keeping out others who aren't like us will make us feel more at home. We can be united or divided by seeking home. At its best, our longing for the Promised Land yearns for everyone to find their promised lands.

We're people called to make our true homes in the heart of God. Yet if our yearning for home is just spiritual, then it's escapist and rightfully disdained by people who live in the real world. The yearning is spiritual and for *what is beyond*—yet also very much for us to have and to ensure everyone has a home *right here and now* for sleeping, getting ready for work, playing, raising children, washing clothes, making dinner. Even when we find home, life is hard. But at least there is a place to struggle from.

After going by the Dead Sea, we continued a short drive in the taxi to where Jesus was baptized in the Jordan River.

All these are places of the Magnificent Story, in which we were kicked out of the garden within the first few pages. By grace God didn't abandon us, but homelessness and searching became immediate, grand themes. Abraham went out, leaving his brother-in-law the better land, to start anew. Jacob slept by the river with a stone for a pillow where he wrestled with God for a blessing. The people exploited in slavery in Egypt's foreign land escaped to freedom. Next, as Joseph told me after I heard how he cared for three orphans and we traded shoes, "The Israelites wandered in the desert for a long time, but God then showed them the way home." Once in their Promised Land, God told them to treat the strangers among them as their own.

The Savior came as a kind of immigrant from heaven, across borders of divinity and time and space, to walk among humanity. Soon after his birth, his family fled as refugees. He grew up and described himself as someone without a place to lay his head. He hung on the cross forsaken by all and then was raised to life. His most influential interpreter traveled to different lands, enduring hardship in and out of prison, in order to tell people that through Jesus they belong to God's chosen people. The end of the story, which we're still living into, is to finally be fully home with God and with people from all corners of the earth.

We care about refugees and immigrants because in so many ways God tells us to and because they're living out the longing of our story. This isn't just being tenderhearted. If this story, the Story of God, is Our Story, then the Christian logic of love demands we help people who are in between, searching, wandering, exiled, seeking home. When we do, helping those without homes brings Home a little closer for all of us by being part of the answer to Jesus' prayer that the kingdom would come, even here, even now.

That kingdom coming happens in part, Jesus says, when we welcome a stranger because then we're welcoming him, the one who is the Way, Truth, and *Life*. Something mystical happens within our practical responses, within the change that happens in the one who is welcomed and in the one who welcomes.

Are we *for* them or *against* them, my son asked back on the first page. We're for them because here is life:

Here is life in overcoming real concerns and fear with truth and love.

Here is life in the aftermath of loss, violence, suffering, and walking away from home for days.

Here is life in then working tenaciously for hope and home.

Here is life because God so welcomes us that we welcome each other.

Here is life because when we welcome strangers we welcome the Life Giver.

Here is life because God's kingdom keeps coming on earth as in heaven.

Here is life when you are very welcomed.

Here is life when you are very welcoming.

Here is a life of love, worth living and worth living together.

✛ ACKNOWLEDGMENTS ✛

The acknowledgments for this book are woven through every page. Thank you to the refugees and immigrants I talked with and read about; to the nonprofit professionals, activists, volunteers, and friends welcoming in the United States and other countries; and to the journalists, researchers, and writers working to inform. Special thanks to Matt Soerens for his leadership in this area and for early guidance toward the right ideas and people. I'm also grateful to the many people I talked with and learned from who aren't on these pages.

I'm grateful to publish a fourth book with InterVarsity Press. Naming names is a problem because I've loved working with everyone there over the past ten years. But on this book I especially thank my editors Cindy Bunch and Ethan McCarthy for insightfully making the book better; the promotion team on this book that includes Helen Lee, Andrew Bronson, and Alisse Wissman; and the publisher, Jeff Crosby, who inspired the idea for this book and has graciously helped lead me from book to book.

I'm grateful to Kathy Helmers, who is both a great agent and a friend with whom I get to learn, grow, and write.

I'm grateful to friends and colleagues: Lance, Jonathan, Norm, and Sandy. Enel and my Haitian colleagues. Jane and Paul and colleagues at DAI. Jamie, Laura, Jenny, and Juana at Wheaton College's Humanitarian Disaster Institute.

Thank you, Shelly. You inspire me daily and helped make this book possible.

Finally, thank you for reading. I'm grateful that together we can strive to make the world more welcoming and loving, because God first loved us.

✤ APPENDIX ✤

Resources and Organizations for Next Steps

I provide a free curriculum for this book and recommend other helpful books and resources for next steps at kentannan.com.

Also, here are some organizations that can provide opportunities for you to take next steps in advocating, giving, or volunteering for refugees and immigrants. It's important to find one that effectively helps those it serves and is a good fit for you. Most of these organizations have ways you can get involved, such as hosting a "Refugee Sunday," giving toward a project, or sponsoring a refugee family.

I'm giving 50 percent of my earnings/royalties from this book to the organizations listed below. Many other good organizations, both local and international, large and small, work with refugees and immigrants. I focus here on larger organizations so there is a good chance you can connect with them wherever you live.

I'm grateful for everyone who serves people in this area with humility, expertise, commitment, and continuous learning.

World Relief

World Relief stands with vulnerable people and partners with local churches to end the cycle of suffering, transform lives, and build sustainable communities. They work both internationally and in the United States, where their work includes resettling refugees. www.worldrelief.org

Lutheran Immigration and Refugee Service

Lutheran Immigration and Refugee Service was established in 1939 by churches in the United States to serve uprooted people during World War II. They work to witness to God's love for all people by standing with and advocating for migrants and refugees.
www.lirs.org

World Vision

World Vision is a Christian organization that has worked in fragile states around the world for over three decades to provide life-saving support and durable solutions for the world's most vulnerable children, which has meant working closely with refugees around the world.
www.worldvision.org

International Rescue Committee

International Rescue Committee was founded in 1933 at the call of Albert Einstein. They are a secular organization with a focus for those whose lives and livelihoods are shattered by conflict and disaster to survive, recover, and regain control of their future. They're committed to research and innovation.
www.rescue.org

World Renew

World Renew is the relief and development organization of the Christian Reformed Church. It responds to the needs of people around the world who are suffering from poverty, hunger, disaster, and injustice, which includes work with refugees both internationally and in North America.
www.worldrenew.net

Caritas

Caritas (Catholic Relief Services) works with local, national, and international partners to assist the poor and vulnerable overseas. It was started by the Catholic Church in the United States seventy-five years ago.
www.caritas.org

Center for Global Development

Center for Global Development works to reduce global poverty and improve lives through innovative economic research that drives better policy and practice by the world's top decision makers. It's vital to have quality research to inform policymakers and the public on refugee and immigration issues.

www.cgdev.org

Humanitarian Disaster Institute (Wheaton College)

Humanitarian Disaster Institute (Wheaton College) is a faith-based academic disaster research center, which is also home of the MA program in humanitarian and disaster leadership that (full disclosure) I lead. The institute's mission is to help the church prepare and care for a disaster-filled world. I'm donating from this book specifically for research projects to serve refugees.

www.wheaton.edu/hdi

I hope these organizations—or one of the many others working to help—can give you a meaningful way to become part of a human chain reaching out to love our neighbors, near and far.

✛ NOTES ✛

1 ARE WE FOR OR AGAINST?

5 *On average, refugees are away*: Xavier Devictor and Quy-Toan Do, "How Many Years Do Refugees Stay in Exile?," Development for Peace, World Bank, September 15, 2016, http://blogs.worldbank.org/dev4peace/how-many-years-do-refugees-stay-exile.

6 *A refugee is*: Definition from the United Nations Refugee Agency's website, www.unrefugees.org/refugee-facts/what-is-a-refugee.

7 *the* Washington Post *told the story*: Robert Samuels, "How to Be an American: Syrian Refugees Find a Home in Trump Country," *Washington Post*, February 5, 2017, www.washingtonpost.com/politics/in-nebraska-syrian-refugees-find-a-warm-and-welcoming-community/2017/02/05/5615c82a-eb9b-11e6-9973-c5efb7ccfb0d_story.html.

An immigrant is: Definition adapted from the United Nations Refugee Agency's website, www.unhcr.org/en-us/news/latest/2016/7/55df0e556/unhcr-viewpoint-refugee-migrant-right.html.

2 THAT COULD BE ME

17 *The famous Milgram psychological study*: Stanley Milgram, "Behavioral Study of Obedience," *Journal of Abnormal and Social Psychology* 67, no. 4 (1963): 371-78, https://doi.org/10.1037%2Fh0040525.

18 *Once you press 15 volts*: These quotes come from Tim Ferriss's interview with Stanford professor emeritus Phil Zimbardo, "How to Not Be Evil—Dr. Phil Zimbardo," *The Tim Ferriss Show*, March 8, 2017, 24:26–26:39, https://castbox.fm/episode/226%3A-How-to-Not-Be-Evil-Dr.-Phil-Zimbardo-id1931-id30074613?country=us. In addition, a large portion of this conversation was helpful for my thinking through this section.

21   *Clarkston, a small town near Atlanta*: Katy Long, "This Small Town in America's Deep South Welcomes 1,500 Refugees a Year," *Guardian*, May 24, 2017, www.theguardian.com/us-news/2017/may/24/clarkston -georgia-refugee-resettlement-program.

22   *What we're doing actually*: "Nigel Farage: 'There Is No Giant Conspiracy' Linked to Meeting with Assange," Fox News Insider, March 12, 2017, http://insider.foxnews.com/2017/03/12/nigel-farage-julian -assange-wikileaks-meeting-donald-trump-conspiracy.

      At crucial moments of choice: Iris Murdoch, *The Sovereignty of Good* (New York: Routledge and Kegan Paul, 1970), 36.

23   *Benedictine monks explicitly try to recognize*: Russell Moore, "Signposts: A Conversation with Rod Dreher," March 10, 2017, https:// www.russellmoore.com/2017/03/10/signposts-conversation-rod -dreher/, podcast conversation between the Southern Baptist Convention's Russell Moore and author Rod Dreher, talking about Benedictine monks.

      Abbot shall pour water: *The Rule of Saint Benedict*, ed. Timothy Fry (Collegeville, MN: Liturgical Press, 1982), 73-74 (emphasis added).

24   *a vigorous vetting process for refugees*: See "U.S. Refugee Admission Program," U.S. Department of State, www.state.gov/j/prm/ra /admissions. And as a more personal description, here is a former immigration officer describing the process: Natasha Hall, "Refugees Are Already Vigorously Vetted. I Know Because I Vetted Them," *Washington Post*, February 1, 2017, www.washingtonpost.com/posteverything /wp/2017/02/01/refugees-are-already-vigorously-vetted-i-know -because-i-vetted-them/?utm.

3 REAL CONCERNS

26   *When Megan's family moved*: "John Crowley—The Real-Life Captain America and Bruce Banner (Seriously)," *The Tim Ferriss Show*, February 28, 2017, 106:15–109:46, https://castbox.fm/episode/225%3A -John-Crowley-The-Real-Life-Captain-America-and-Bruce-Banner -(Seriously)-id1059468-id51930636?country=us.

28   *It strikes me that if what*: Ben Mauk, "102 Villagers, 750 Refugees, One Grand Experiment," *Guardian*, April 19, 2017, www.theguardian.com /news/2017/apr/19/102-villagers-750-refugees-one-grand-experiment.

29   *White people will have quite enough*: James Baldwin, quoted in "Nation: The Root of the Negro Problem," *Time*, May 17, 1963, http://content .time.com/time/subscriber/article/0,33009,830326-2,00.html.

30   *refugees brought in $63 billion more:* "Rejected Report Shows Revenue Brought in by Refugees," *New York Times,* September 19, 2017, www.nytimes.com/interactive/2017/09/19/us/politics/document-Refugee -Report.html.

refugees are paying more in taxes: Matthew Soerens, "Will America Stand Again With the World's Refugees?," *New York Times,* January 26, 2018, https://www.nytimes.com/2018/01/26/opinion/will-america -stand-again-with-the-worlds-refugees.html.

these workers help the economy: Ana Swanson, "The Big Myth About Refugees," *Washington Post,* September 10, 2015, www.washingtonpost .com/news/wonk/wp/2015/09/10/the-big-myth-about-refugees/?utm.

31   *For an American:* Alex Nowrasteh, "Terrorism and Immigration: A Risk Analysis," Policy Analysis no. 798, Cato Institute, September 13, 2016, www.cato.org/publications/policy-analysis/terrorism-immigration -risk-analysis.

32   *Incidentally, white men commit the majority:* Mark Follman, Gavin Aronsen, and Deanna Pan, "US Mass Shootings, 1982-2018: Data from Mother Jones' Investigation," *Mother Jones,* updated March 10, 2018, www .motherjones.com/politics/2012/12/mass-shootings-mother-jones -full-data/.

the presence of more immigrants: See, for example, the studies cited in these articles: Eyal Press, "Trump and the Truth: Immigration and Crime," *New Yorker,* September 2, 2016, www.newyorker.com/news /news-desk/trump-and-the-truth-immigration-and-crime, and Ana Flagg, "The Myth of the Criminal Immigrant," *New York Times,* March 30, 2018, www.nytimes.com/interactive/2018/03/30/upshot /crime-immigration-myth.html.

The vetting process: "U.S. Refugee Admissions Program," U.S. Department of State, www.state.gov/j/prm/ra/admissions.

the odds of being an American killed: Alex Nowrasteh, "Terrorism and Immigration: A Risk Analysis," Policy Analysis no. 798, Cato Institute, September 13, 2016, https://www.cato.org/publications/policy-analysis /terrorism-immigration-risk-analysis.

33   *There is evidence:* Michael Clemens, "The Real Economic Cost of Accepting Refugees," Center for Global Development, September 14, 2017, www.cgdev.org/blog/real-economic-cost-accepting-refugees.

34   *Belonging to society requires sacrifice:* Sebastian Junger, *Tribe: On Homecoming and Belonging* (New York: Twelve, 2016), 133.

35   *Even if the country gets overcrowded*: "The Ungrateful Refugee: 'We Have No Debt to Repay,'" *The Guardian*, April 4, 2017, www.theguardian .com/world/2017/apr/04/dina-nayeri-ungrateful-refugee.

36   *change like this in Androscoggin County*: Claire Galofaro, "How a Community Changed by Refugees Came to Embrace Trump," Associated Press, April 19, 2017, https://apnews.com/7f2b534b80674596875980b 9b6e701c9.

      I often think of America as a lifeboat: "Antonio Vargas: Define American," *Real Time with Bill Maher* (HBO series), April 3, 2017, https://www .youtube.com/watch?v=SPBtCIGpl5M.

37   *societies also correctly maintain their integrity*: John Stackhouse, "The Bible Says to Welcome the Stranger—or Does It?," Context with Lorna Dueck, http://www.contextwithlornadueck.com/2017/02/08 /the-bible-says-to-welcome-the-stranger-or-does-it/.

      We should welcome more refugees: Matthew Soerens, "Will America Stand Again with the World's Refugees?," *New York Times*, January 26, 2018, www.nytimes.com/2018/01/26/opinion/will-america-stand -again-with-the-worlds-refugees.html.

42   *Behind me, I heard the same man*: Elie Wiesel, *Night*, trans. Marion Wiesel (New York: Hill and Wang, 2006), 65.

43   *Where I was most proud*: "John Crowley—The Real-Life Captain America and Bruce Banner (Seriously)," 58:22–1:00:22.

4 THIS IS OUR STORY

47   *Immigration wasn't an option*: Harry Radliffe II, "Sir Nicholas Winton 'Saving the Children,'" *60 Minutes*, July 2, 2015, available on CBS All Access and at https://www.youtube.com/watch?v=c0aoifNziKQ.

48   *I'm not sure it's possible to tell*: Ben Mauk, "102 Villagers, 750 Refugees, One Grand Experiment," *Guardian*, April 19, 2017, www.theguardian.com /news/2017/apr/19/102-villagers-750-refugees-one-grand-experiment.

49   *If it is a dehumanizing lie*: Mauk, "102 Villagers."

      You stand on the shore just before dawn: I based this narrative on stories from the compelling book by Patrick Kingsley, *The New Odyssey* (New York: Liveright Publishing, 2017).

51   *On Tuesday morning as your dad*: This story is based on Lindsey Bever and Ed O'Keefe, "A 13-Year-Old Sobbed on Camera When ICE Took

Her Father Away. Now She Has a Plan," *Washington Post*, March 29, 2017, www.washingtonpost.com/news/post-nation/wp/2017/03/29/a-13-year-old-sobbed-on-camera-when-ice-took-her-father-away-now-she-has-a-plan/?utm.

54 *As of the end:* Xavier Devictor and Quy-Toan Do, "How Many Years Do Refugees Stay in Exile?," The World Bank, September 15, 2016, http://blogs.worldbank.org/dev4peace/how-many-years-do-refugees-stay-exile.

55 *Most refugees stay:* Mark Leon Goldberg, "The Trump Administration Will Dramatically Lower Refugee Admittance Based on a Totally False Premise," UN Dispatch, September 26, 2017, www.undispatch.com/trump-administration-will-dramatically-lower-refugee-admittance-based-totally-false-premise/?utm.

A study a couple of years ago: "Evangelical Views on Immigration," LifeWay Research, February 2015, http://lifewayresearch.com/wp-content/uploads/2015/03/Evangelical-Views-on-Immigration-Report.pdf.

56 *We've got a lot of white nationalists:* Esther Choo on Twitter: @choo_ek, August 16, 2017. I edited the punctuation between tweets for flow.

58 *how the category "white" has been used:* See also *The History of White People* by Nell Irvin Painter and Thomas Rogers's interview with Painter, "'The History of White People': What It Means to Be White," *Salon*, March 23, 2010, www.salon.com/2010/03/23/history_of_white_people_nell_irvin_painter.

60 *part of a Magnificent Story:* James Bryan Smith, *The Magnificent Story: Uncovering a Gospel of Beauty Goodness, and Truth* (Downers Grove, IL: InterVarsity Press, 2017).

5 GETTING PRACTICAL

66 *the London marathon:* Callum Davis, "London Marathon Runner Gives Up His Own Race to Help Exhausted Athlete in Ultimate Act of Sportsmanship," *Telegraph*, April 23, 2017, www.telegraph.co.uk/athletics/2017/04/23/london-marathon-runner-gives-race-help-exhausted-athlete-ultimate/.

67 *My calf started to cramp:* Davis, "London Marathon Runner."

74 *we should partner* with *people:* See the chapter on partnering (chap. 5) in my *Slow Kingdom Coming* (Downers Grove, IL: InterVarsity Press, 2016).

74   *We count the partnering cost:* My Haitian friend and colleague Enel Angervil has taught me about this, and since he and his country are often on the receiving end of help from other people, he often takes the chance to share with foreigners the passage from Luke 14:28: "Which of you, intending to build a tower, does not first sit down and estimate the cost, to see whether he has enough to complete it?"

75   *In the United States:* Michael Clemens, "The Real Economic Cost of Accepting Refugees," Center for Global Development, September 14, 2017, www.cgdev.org/blog/real-economic-cost-accepting-refugees.

76   *About 1 million:* Gustavo López and Kristen Bialik, "Key Findings about U.S. Immigrants," Pew Research Center, May 3, 2017, www.pewresearch .org/fact-tank/2017/05/03/key-findings-about-u-s-immigrants/?utm.

      darkness went with them: J. R. R. Tolkien, "Of the Rings of Power and the Third Age," in *The Silmarillion,* 2nd ed. (New York: Del Rey, 1977), 346.

78   *Another refugee resettlement agency:* Lutheran Immigration and Refugee Service, "Our Work," www.lirs.org/our-work.

79   *I saw a couple of people:* See video in this BBC report, "London Marathon Runner Helps Struggling Rival to Finish," April 23, 2017, www.bbc.com /news/av/uk-wales-39686037/london-marathon-runner-helps -struggling-rival-to-finish.

6 FORM A HUMAN CHAIN

83   *Mike McClendhan's church:* Solana Beach Prebyterian Church is in Solana Beach, California.

      Welcoming the Stranger: Matt Soerens and Jenny Yang, *Welcoming the Stranger: Justice, Compassion & Truth in the Immigration Debate,* revised and expanded (Downers Grove, IL: InterVarsity Press, 2018).

84   *Our national immigration situation:* Gustavo López and Kristen Bialik, "Key Findings About U.S. Immigrants," Pew Research Center, May 3, 2017, www.pewresearch.org/fact-tank/2017/05/03/key-findings -about-u-s-immigrants/?utm.

85   *Research of the past:* Robert Adelman et al., "Urban Crime Rates and the Changing Face of Immigration: Evidence across Four Decades," Journal of Ethnicity in Criminal Justice 15 (2017): 52-77.

86   *the conference in Uganda:* I was traveling with Development Associates International (DAI), a Christian nonprofit based in Colorado Springs that serves through leadership development in dozens of countries around the world.

87   *My daughter . . . had passionate opinions*: "Heartbreaking Generosity: Heather Heyer's Dad Speaks About Forgiveness," The Majority Report with Sam Seder, August 15, 2017, https://www.youtube.com/watch?v=dPFCfoTReF4.

90   *We'll rise up*: Andra Day, "Rise Up," *Cheers to the Fall*, Warner Bros./ Buskin, 2015.

7 HERE IS LIFE

100   *It was amazing how many people*: This quotation and a number of details in this section are from Vincent McDermott, "Syrian Refugee Gives Birth Hours After Landing in Fort McMurray," *Edmonton Journal*, February 2, 2017, http://edmontonjournal.com/news/local-news/syrian-refugee-gives-birth-hours-after-landing-in-fort-mcmurray.

101   *sympathy . . . and empathy*: The scholar Brené Brown in her books and lectures goes into helpful detail about these ideas.

103   *I read a* New York Times *article*: Dionne Searcey, "Fleeing Boko Haram, Thousands Cling to a Road to Nowhere," *New York Times*, March 30, 2017, www.nytimes.com/interactive/2017/03/30/world/africa/the-road-to-nowhere-niger.html.

104   *Juan came to this country as a child*: Kate Shellnutt, "Evangelicals to Trump: Don't Deport Our Next Generation of Church Leaders," *Christianity Today*, September 1, 2017, www.christianitytoday.com/news/2017/september/evangelicals-to-trump-dont-deport-dreamers-daca-immigration.html.

       Recently in Fairfax County, Virginia: Julie Zauzmer, "An Anti-Muslim Slur on Their Wall Made This Family Think of Leaving the U.S. Then Neighbors Came to Their Aid," *Washington Post*, March 31, 2017, www.washingtonpost.com/news/acts-of-faith/wp/2017/03/31/a-hate-crime-made-this-muslim-family-think-of-leaving-the-country-then-neighbors-came-to-their-aid/?utm.

105   *My friend Gustave came to the United States*: I wrote about their family in my book *After Shock: Searching for Honest Faith When Your World Is Shaken* (Downers Grove, IL: InterVarsity Press, 2011), 9-15, 83-84, 113-15, 123-29.

ABOUT THE AUTHOR

***K*ent Annan** (MDiv, Princeton Theological Seminary) is director of humanitarian and disaster leadership at Wheaton College, where he provides leadership to the MA program within the Humanitarian Disaster Institute. He is the author of *Slow Kingdom Coming*, *After Shock*, and *Following Jesus Through the Eye of the Needle*.

He worked for two years in western Europe with refugees from Bosnia, Iran, Sierra Leone, and many other countries. He later worked for six months with refugees in Albania and then in Kosovo.

Kent is a senior consultant at Development Associates International, which trains Christian leaders around the world. He cofounded Haiti Partners, lived in Haiti for two and a half years, and spent fifteen years working on education with churches in Haiti. He is on the board of Equitas Group, a philanthropic organization that seeks justice for the vulnerable and encourages holistic thinking about justice.

Kent speaks regularly to groups around the country and teaches adult education at his local church. He is married to Shelly. They have a daughter, Simone, and son, Cormac.

For more about Kent, to invite him to speak, or to find resources related to *You Welcomed Me*, visit kentannan.com.

OTHER BOOKS
BY KENT ANNAN

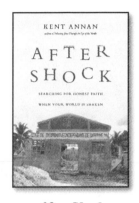

Slow Kingdom Coming
Practices for Doing
Justice, Loving Mercy
and Walking Humbly in
the World

After Shock
Searching for Honest
Faith When Your World
Is Shaken

**Following Jesus Through
the Eye of the Needle**
Living Fully, Loving
Dangerously